Dillard's Presents

Southern Living Christmas COOKBOOK

RONALD MCDONALD
HOUSE CHARITIES

Benefiting Ronald McDonald House Charities

Peppermint Cake with Seven-Minute Frosting *recipe on page 73.*

RONALD McDONALD
HOUSE CHARITIES

Merry Christmas
from all your friends at Dillard's!

We are proud to support the
Ronald McDonald House.

The purchase of this book helps families of seriously ill
children stay in a comfortable haven near their children.

Proceeds go to Ronald McDonald Houses in local
communities to help families in need.

Thank you for your generosity.

May your family have a wonderful holiday season and
a healthy and prosperous 2020.

CONTENTS

 Icon indicates total time is under 1 hour.

HOLIDAY STYLE

For a warm and welcoming entrance, a festive table, a comfy room for holiday guests, and more, look no further than these bright ideas and decorations to deck your halls with cheer. All products shown are from the Southern Living Collection, exclusively at Dillard's.

Noel

DON THE DOOR

A warm welcome to holiday visitors starts at the front door. ❶ The contrast between natural materials in earthy tones—a grapevine wreath and garland of greenery studded with pine cones and dusty-green leaves, plus accent pieces in silver and gold—makes for a striking presentation. To make the "lanterns," loosely wrap strings of battery-powered LED fairy garden lights into balls and place them in wooden boxes or crates with mesh sides. ❷ A barnboard sign propped up on one side of the door wishes guests a merry "NOEL." A swag of greenery entwined with a beaded garland and tree toppers in galvanized buckets create a mini forest at the entrance. ❸ A nearly life-size nutcracker planter welcomes guests with a bit of greenery and a friendly face. ❹ "Little drummer" planters fitted with lit-up small trees give this front porch a bit of sparkle. Year-round pillows on the porch swing are swapped out for some in cherry plaid and one bearing the message of the season. A throw keeps guests warm and cozy.

TRIM THE TREE

The key to a showstopping tree is to pick a color theme and apply it on multiple levels and in various spots throughout the room. ❶ A gold-suited Santa stands sentry next to the tree while a silver reindeer looks on. ❷ Glass ornaments in silver, gold, and frosty white with pops of cranberry-red set the tone. ❸ Stockings in snow-white and scarlet provide a crisp contrast in color. ❹ The tree is elegant but has an air of casualness. Instead of a star, it's crowned with a profusion of metallic leaves.

GATHER 'ROUND

❶ Cocktails served on a pretty tray kick off the party on a spirited note. ❷ At this cookie and cocoa station, holiday-theme linens, mugs, and a tiered serving tray serve up the sweets while a silvery wreath adds sparkle. ❸ Nostalgia reigns in this place setting. Place mats in red-and-white-striped ticking provide the underpinning for a wooden charger, a red dinner plate, and a salad plate painted with a snowy rural scene. ❹ Adorable puppy plates greet dinner guests at this whimsically set table.

BEAUTY REST

Freshen up your guest room with new bed linens and pillows. ❶ A red reindeer pillow adds a spark of color to sage-green and white Scandinavian-style bedding. ❷ A Fair Isle-style comforter in shades of creamy white and taupe provides a foundation for this red-and-white bedding ensemble. ❸ Extra pillows in different shades of Buffalo plaid encourage guests to build up a spot for sitting up in bed. ❹ A comfy chair decked out with holiday-theme pillows and a soft throw trimmed in furry tassels create a cozy spot for reading. ❺ A mix of red and white in ticking, plaids, plain white, and Fair Isle patterns creates a crisp and wintry theme that can be left in place all year.

HOLIDAY RECIPES

Spinach, Beet, and Orange Salad
with Walnut Vinaigrette *recipe on page 22*

HOLIDAY SIDES

These sublime supporting dishes deserve star status.
Serve alongside a piece of protein for a weekday meal anytime of year.

Root Ribbon Salad with
Warm Honey Vinaigrette

ROOT RIBBON SALAD WITH WARM HONEY VINAIGRETTE

The long leaves of Lacinato kale are dark and glossy and more tender than curly kale, making them ideal for salads. A trick for making root vegetable ribbons: Peel a long, straight ribbon from one side of a carrot or parsnip so that it can lie flat on the work surface. Holding the vegetable steady against the surface, shave even ribbons from the top with a vegetable peeler.

SERVES 6 **HANDS-ON** 25 MINUTES **TOTAL** 1 HOUR

1 bunch Lacinato kale (about 7 ounces), stemmed

3 carrots (about 14 ounces), peeled

2 parsnips (about 6 ounces), peeled

¼ cup extra-virgin olive oil

1 medium shallot, finely chopped (about 3 tablespoons)

2 tablespoons balsamic vinegar

1 tablespoon honey

¾ teaspoon kosher salt

½ teaspoon black pepper

4 ounces Parmesan cheese, shaved (about ½ cup)

1 cup glazed pecans, chopped

1 Cut the kale into ½-inch strips to equal 2½ cups. Shave the carrots and parsnips into ribbons with a vegetable peeler. Combine the kale, carrots, and parsnips in a large bowl.

2 Heat 1 tablespoon of the olive oil in a small saucepan over medium. Add the chopped shallot, and cook, stirring often, until translucent, about 3 minutes. Add the balsamic vinegar, and cook until slightly thickened, about 2 minutes. Add the honey, salt, and pepper, and swirl until incorporated. Stir in the remaining 3 tablespoons olive oil.

3 Add the warm dressing to the kale mixture, tossing gently to combine. Top with the shaved Parmesan and chopped glazed pecans.

SPINACH, BEET, AND ORANGE SALAD WITH WALNUT VINAIGRETTE

Oranges add bright color, flavor, and texture to the traditional beet and goat cheese salad. Test the beets with a paring knife before taking them out of the foil. If they are difficult to pierce, give them a little more time in the oven. Photo page 18.

SERVES 10 **HANDS-ON** 15 MINUTES **TOTAL** 1 HOUR, 40 MINUTES

2   large red beets (about 1 pound)
2   tablespoons walnut oil
2   tablespoons extra-virgin olive oil
2   tablespoons red wine vinegar
1   teaspoon Dijon mustard
¾   teaspoon kosher salt
½   teaspoon black pepper
4   cups fresh baby spinach (about 5 ounces)
2   cups chopped frisée (about 4 ounces)
1   navel orange, peeled and sectioned
¼   cup chopped toasted walnuts
4   ounces goat cheese, broken into large pieces (about ½ cup)
2   tablespoons chopped fresh flat-leaf parsley

1 Preheat the oven to 425°F. Wrap the beets in aluminum foil, and place on a foil-lined rimmed baking sheet. Bake in the preheated oven until tender, 45 minutes to 1 hour. Remove the foil, and let the beets stand until cool enough to handle, about 10 minutes. Peel the beets, and chop into 1-inch pieces. Let cool completely, about 30 minutes.

2 Whisk together the walnut oil, olive oil, vinegar, Dijon, ½ teaspoon of the salt, and ¼ teaspoon of the pepper in a small bowl until blended and smooth. Toss together the chopped beets, 2½ tablespoons of the vinaigrette, and the remaining ¼ teaspoon each salt and pepper in a medium bowl.

3 Gently toss the spinach and frisée with the remaining vinaigrette. Place the greens mixture on a platter, and top with the beet mixture, orange sections, walnuts, goat cheese, and parsley. Serve immediately.

CAST-IRON CIPOLLINI ONIONS WITH MAPLE AND SHERRY

The onions take a little work, but the payoff is sweet. Photo page 24.

SERVES 6 **HANDS-ON** 30 MINUTES **TOTAL** 30 MINUTES

2 pounds cipollini onions
1 tablespoon canola oil
¼ cup sherry vinegar
1 teaspoon kosher salt
½ teaspoon black pepper
3 tablespoons strong brewed coffee
2 tablespoons pure maple syrup
2 tablespoons unsalted butter
1 tablespoon chopped fresh thyme

1 Bring a large saucepan of water to a boil. Trim the roots and stems of the onions, and cook in the boiling water 45 seconds. Transfer to a large bowl of ice water; let stand 1 minute. Gently remove the skins from the onions; dry the onions on paper towels.

2 Heat the canola oil in a large cast-iron skillet over medium-high. Add the onions, and cook, stirring occasionally, until lightly browned, about 3 minutes on each side. Add the sherry vinegar, salt, and pepper, and bring to a simmer. Cook, stirring occasionally, until the liquid has reduced slightly, about 2 minutes. Add the coffee and maple syrup, and cook, stirring occasionally, until the liquid thickens to a sauce consistency, about 5 minutes. Add the butter, stirring until the butter melts and the sauce is velvety and thick, about 2 minutes. Sprinkle with the thyme, and serve immediately.

Shaved Brussels Sprouts with Pancetta and Smoked Almonds
recipe on page 27

Cast-Iron Cipollini Onions with Maple and Sherry
recipe on page 23

**Farro and Wild
Mushroom Casserole**
recipe on page 28

**Celery Root, Apple,
and Potato Gratin**
recipe on page 29

WINTER GREENS TART

If a vegetarian dish can stick to your ribs, this is it. Gooey goodness binds greens and creamy eggs.
A sliver is a lovely side. A wedge is a hearty meal.

SERVES 8 HANDS-ON 30 MINUTES **TOTAL** 2 HOURS, 30 MINUTES

TART DOUGH

- 1¼ cups (about 5⅜ ounces) all-purpose flour, plus more to flour surface
- ½ teaspoon granulated sugar
- ½ teaspoon kosher salt
- 6 tablespoons cold unsalted butter, cubed
- 4 to 5 tablespoons ice water

FILLING

- 2 tablespoons extra-virgin olive oil
- ½ cup diced shallots (from 2 small or 1 large)
- 3 garlic cloves, minced
- ½ pound turnip greens, stemmed and chopped
- ½ pound mustard greens, stemmed and chopped
- ½ teaspoon granulated sugar
- 3 large eggs
- ¾ cup half-and-half
- 2 ounces Gruyère cheese, finely shredded
- 1 teaspoon kosher salt
- ½ teaspoon black pepper
- ⅛ teaspoon freshly grated nutmeg

1 Prepare the Tart Dough: Pulse the flour, sugar, and salt in a food processor until combined, 3 or 4 times. Add the butter; pulse until it resembles coarse meal. With the processor running, add the water, 1 tablespoon at a time; process until a ball forms and pulls away from the sides of the bowl. Turn the dough out onto a work surface, gather into a ball, and flatten into a disk. Wrap in plastic and refrigerate until firm, about 1 hour.

2 Preheat the oven to 350°F. Unwrap the dough, and place on a floured surface. Roll into an 11-inch circle (¼ inch thick). Fit the dough into a 9-inch tart pan with a removable bottom; trim edges, discarding excess. Prick the bottom of crust with a fork to let steam escape while baking. Freeze the dough in the tart pan 15 minutes.

3 Remove the tart pan from the freezer; line the dough with parchment, and fill with pie weights. Bake at 350°F until edges begin to brown, about 20 minutes. Remove the weights and parchment; bake until bottom is browned, 13 minutes. Cool on a wire rack, 15 minutes.

4 Prepare the Filling: Heat the oil in a large skillet over medium-high. Add the shallots, and cook, stirring often, until translucent, about 3 minutes. Add the garlic, and cook, stirring often, 1 minute. Stir in the greens; cover and cook until tender, about 5 minutes. Uncover, sprinkle with sugar, and cook, stirring occasionally, until all liquid has evaporated, about 2 minutes. Transfer to a colander, pressing lightly to remove any excess moisture.

5 Whisk together the eggs, half-and-half, cheese, salt, pepper, and nutmeg in a large bowl. Add the greens, and stir to combine. Pour the Filling into prepared Tart Dough in pan, and bake at 350°F until just set, about 30 minutes. Cool on a wire rack 15 minutes before serving.

SHAVED BRUSSELS SPROUTS WITH PANCETTA AND SMOKED ALMONDS

Peppery pancetta is an Italian cured, not smoked, version of bacon. It's the almonds that add the smoky element to this delightful side dish. Photo page 24.

SERVES 6 **HANDS-ON** 20 MINUTES **TOTAL** 30 MINUTES

6   ounces diced pancetta (about 1¼ cups)

1¼   pounds Brussels sprouts, trimmed and shaved (about 5 cups)

⅓   cup coarsely chopped smoked almonds (about 2 ounces)

⅓   cup dried currants (about 1½ ounces)

¼   cup apple cider vinegar

1   tablespoon extra-virgin olive oil

1   tablespoon honey

2   teaspoons Dijon mustard

½   teaspoon kosher salt

½   teaspoon black pepper

1   Cook the pancetta in a small skillet over medium, stirring occasionally, until crisp, 8 to 10 minutes. Transfer the pancetta to a plate lined with paper towels, reserving 3 tablespoons drippings.

2   Combine the Brussels sprouts, almonds, currants, and pancetta in a large bowl, tossing to combine.

3   Whisk together the cider vinegar, olive oil, honey, Dijon mustard, salt, pepper, and the reserved 3 tablespoons pancetta drippings in a small bowl until blended and smooth. Pour over the Brussels sprouts mixture, and toss gently.

FARRO AND WILD MUSHROOM CASSEROLE

This casserole was a side dish hit at the Test Kitchen table. Photo page 25.

SERVES 8 TO 10 **HANDS-ON** 25 MINUTES **TOTAL** 1 HOUR, 10 MINUTES

2   cups water
1   cup uncooked pearled farro
½   pound Swiss chard with stems
3   tablespoons extra-virgin olive oil
8   ounces shiitake mushrooms, stemmed and sliced (about 3¼ cups)
8   ounces cremini mushrooms, sliced (about 3¼ cups)
1   teaspoon kosher salt
1   large carrot, peeled and diced (about 1½ cups)
½   large yellow onion, diced (about 1½ cups)
1½ cups mushroom broth (such as Pacific)
¼   cup dry white wine
¼   cup salted butter
3   tablespoons all-purpose flour
4   ounces Parmesan cheese, grated (about 1 cup)
½   cup panko (Japanese-style breadcrumbs)
¼   cup chopped fresh flat-leaf parsley

1 Preheat the oven to 400°F. Bring the water and farro to a boil in a saucepan over high. Reduce the heat to low; simmer until tender, 20 minutes. Drain.

2 Finely chop the chard stems to equal 2 cups. Roughly chop the leaves to equal 3½ cups. Heat the oil in a large ovenproof skillet over medium-high. Add the mushrooms and salt; cook, stirring occasionally, until browned, about 8 minutes. Add the carrot, onion, and chard stems; cook, stirring often, until tender, about 5 minutes. Add the chopped chard leaves and ¼ cup broth; cover. Cook until wilted, 3 to 4 minutes.

3 Uncover the skillet; add the wine, stirring to loosen the browned bits from the bottom. Simmer until the liquid has evaporated, about 1 minute. Stir in 3 tablespoons of the butter; cook until melted. Sprinkle the flour over the mixture, stirring constantly. Gradually add the remaining 1¼ cups mushroom broth, ½ cup at a time, stirring to incorporate. Bring mixture to a simmer, and cook, stirring often, until thickened, about 2 minutes. Remove from the heat, and stir in the cheese and cooked farro.

4 Melt the remaining 1 tablespoon butter and toss with the panko. Sprinkle the panko mixture over the farro in the skillet. Transfer to the oven; bake until edges are bubbly, about 30 minutes. Remove and sprinkle with parsley. Let stand 10 minutes before serving.

CELERY ROOT, APPLE, AND POTATO GRATIN

Earthy, sweet, and creamy, this dish is a twist on the traditional potato gratin. Photo page 25.

....

SERVES 8 **HANDS-ON** 25 MINUTES **TOTAL** 1 HOUR, 35 MINUTES

2 tablespoons unsalted butter

1½ cups heavy cream

1¼ teaspoons kosher salt

½ teaspoon black pepper

½ cup toasted hazelnuts

½ cup panko (Japanese-style breadcrumbs)

2 medium-size russet potatoes, peeled and thinly sliced (about 1½ pounds)

1 large celery root, peeled and thinly sliced (about 24 ounces)

1 large Fuji apple, peeled and thinly sliced (about 8 ounces)

12 ounces aged white Cheddar cheese, shredded (about 1½ cups)

1 Preheat the oven to 400°F.

2 Cook the butter in a small saucepan over medium, stirring often, until the butter is browned and has a nutty aroma, about 5 minutes. Let cool slightly, about 3 minutes.

3 Whisk together the cream, salt, and pepper in a medium bowl.

4 Pulse the hazelnuts in a food processor until coarsely chopped. Stir together the chopped hazelnuts, panko, and browned butter in a small bowl until combined.

5 Arrange one-third of the potato, celery root, and Fuji apple slices in a single layer over the bottom of a 3-quart baking dish. Pour one-third of the cream mixture over the top, and sprinkle with about ½ cup of the cheese. Repeat the procedure once. Layer the remaining potato, celery root, and apple slices on top, and sprinkle with the remaining ½ cup cheese. Pour the remaining cream mixture over the casserole, and sprinkle with the panko mixture.

6 Cover the baking dish with aluminum foil, and bake in the preheated oven until the vegetables are softened, about 45 minutes. Remove the foil, and bake, uncovered, until the panko is golden brown, about 15 more minutes. Remove from the oven, and let cool slightly before serving, 10 to 15 minutes.

ROOT VEGETABLE RATATOUILLE

This is a wintry version of the French Provençal summer classic.

SERVES 6 **HANDS-ON** 25 MINUTES **TOTAL** 45 MINUTES

4   tablespoons extra-virgin olive oil
2   cups cubed peeled butternut
    squash (from 1 medium squash)
2   cups cubed peeled rutabaga (from
    1 large rutabaga)
2   cups cubed peeled parsnips (from
    4 medium parsnips)
2   cups cubed peeled sweet potato
    (from 1 medium potato)
1½ teaspoons kosher salt
1   teaspoon black pepper
3   tablespoons (1½ ounces) brandy
1   cup chicken stock
¼   cup salted butter
3   teaspoons fresh thyme leaves
    Garnishes: fresh thyme leaves
    (optional)

1   Heat the oil in a high-sided skillet over medium-high. Add the squash, rutabaga, parsnips, and sweet potato. Cook, stirring occasionally, until lightly browned on all sides, about 6 to 8 minutes. Sprinkle with the salt and pepper. Reduce the heat to medium-low; cover and cook, stirring occasionally, until tender, 10 to 15 minutes.

2   Uncover skillet, increase heat to medium-high, and add the brandy, stirring to loosen browned bits from the bottom of skillet. Cook 1 minute. Add the stock, increase heat to high, and cook until liquid has mostly evaporated, about 3 minutes. Remove from the heat, and stir in the butter and thyme. Serve immediately. Garnish, if desired.

Root Vegetable Ratatouille

Braised Leeks with Fried Capers *recipe on page 34*

Sorghum-Glazed Turnips *recipe on page 37*

Winter Baked Beans *recipe on page 36*

Smashed Fingerlings with Butter and Sage *recipe on page 35*

BRAISED LEEKS WITH FRIED CAPERS

Fried capers add a welcome crunch to meltingly tender leeks. Photo page 32.

SERVES 12 **HANDS-ON** 20 MINUTES **TOTAL** 45 MINUTES

2   tablespoons, plus ¼ cup canola oil
6   medium leeks, rinsed, halved lengthwise, tough outer layers removed, and tops trimmed
½   cup dry white wine
½   teaspoon kosher salt
½   teaspoon black pepper
¾   cup vegetable stock
1   teaspoon lemon zest, plus 2 teaspoons fresh juice (from 1 lemon)
¼   cup capers, drained
2   tablespoons chopped fresh flat-leaf parsley

1   Heat 2 tablespoons of the canola oil in a large cast-iron skillet over medium-high. Add the leeks, cut sides down, in a single layer. Cook until lightly golden, about 4 minutes. Turn the leeks, and cook until the leeks begin to become tender, about 3 minutes. Turn the leeks back to cut sides down.

2   Add the wine, salt, and pepper, and stir gently to loosen the browned bits from the bottom of the skillet, keeping leeks in a single layer. Cook until the liquid is reduced by half (about ¼ cup). Add the vegetable stock, and bring the liquid to a boil. Cover, reduce the heat to medium-low, and simmer until the leeks are softened, about 15 minutes. Uncover and simmer until completely tender, about 10 minutes. Increase the heat to high, and cook until the liquid has thickened slightly and reduced by half (about ¼ cup), about 2 minutes. Stir in the lemon juice, and keep warm.

3   Heat the remaining ¼ cup oil in a 10-inch skillet over medium-high. Fry the capers in hot oil, stirring often, until the capers are crispy and burst open, about 2 minutes. Using a slotted spoon, transfer the capers to a plate lined with paper towels to drain. Combine the parsley, lemon zest, and capers in a small bowl. Sprinkle over the leeks, and serve immediately.

SMASHED FINGERLINGS WITH BUTTER AND SAGE

Waxy fingerlings add interest to this toothsome smash that's loaded with flavor. Photo page 33.

SERVES 6 **HANDS-ON** 35 MINUTES **TOTAL** 55 MINUTES

2   quarts water
½   cup white vinegar
½   tablespoon kosher salt
1½ pounds fingerling potatoes (about 18 potatoes)
1   cup unsalted butter
3   garlic cloves, smashed
¼   cup fresh sage leaves
4   ounces Parmigiano-Reggiano cheese, finely shredded (about 1 cup)
1   teaspoon flaky sea salt (such as Maldon)
½   teaspoon black pepper

1 Preheat the oven to 500°F.

2 Bring the water, vinegar, and kosher salt to a boil in a large saucepan over high. Add the potatoes, and cook until just tender, about 20 minutes. Drain the potatoes, and let cool slightly, about 3 minutes.

3 Heat the butter, garlic, and 3 tablespoons of the sage leaves in a small saucepan over medium until the butter is melted; remove from heat. Chop the remaining sage leaves, and reserve for garnish.

4 Place the potatoes on a work surface, and gently flatten using the bottom of a heavy saucepan or skillet. Line 2 rimmed baking sheets with parchment paper, and lightly grease with cooking spray. Transfer the smashed potatoes to the prepared baking sheets. Brush tops of potatoes with some of the melted butter mixture. Reserve the remaining butter mixture in pan. Bake potatoes in the preheated oven until slightly golden around edges, 6 to 8 minutes. Rotate the pans, turn the potatoes over, and sprinkle with ½ cup of the cheese. Bake until the cheese is browned and potatoes are crispy around the edges, about 5 to 7 minutes.

5 Meanwhile, cook the reserved butter mixture in the saucepan over medium until browned and toasty.

6 Place the potatoes on a platter, drizzle with cooked butter mixture, and sprinkle with reserved chopped sage, sea salt, pepper, and the remaining ½ cup of cheese.

WINTER BAKED BEANS

White beans, sausage, and dark ale combine in this hearty bean casserole topped with crumbled cornbread. Photo page 33.

SERVES 12 **HANDS-ON** 45 MINUTES **TOTAL** 1 HOUR

1   tablespoon extra-virgin olive oil
½   pound andouille sausage, chopped
6   garlic cloves, minced (about 2 tablespoons)
2   celery stalks, diced (about 1 cup)
1   red bell pepper, diced (about 2 cups)
1   small yellow onion, diced (about 1½ cups)
3   (15-ounce) cans cannellini beans, drained and rinsed
1   (12-ounce) bottle brown ale (such as Newcastle)
3   tablespoons light brown sugar
2   tablespoons apple cider vinegar
1   bay leaf
1   teaspoon hot sauce
1½ teaspoons kosher salt
1   teaspoon black pepper
2   cups large cornbread crumbles
1   tablespoon chopped fresh flat-leaf parsley
    Cooking spray

1 Heat the oil in a large Dutch oven or deep cast-iron skillet over medium-high. Add sausage, and cook, stirring often, until heated through and crisp, about 8 minutes. Add the garlic, celery, bell pepper, and onion, and cook, stirring often, until tender, about 5 minutes. Stir in the cannellini beans, ale, brown sugar, vinegar, bay leaf, hot sauce, salt, and black pepper, and bring to a boil. Reduce the heat to medium-low, and simmer, stirring occasionally, until tender, 30 to 40 minutes. Spoon into an 11×7-inch baking dish; discard the bay leaf.

2 Preheat the broiler with oven rack 8 inches from heat.

3 Sprinkle the cornbread crumbles and parsley over the bean mixture, and coat topping with cooking spray. Broil until the cornbread is lightly browned and crispy, 2 to 3 minutes.

SORGHUM-GLAZED TURNIPS

Sorghum syrup and bourbon add a distinctive Southern note to this winter root.
Photo page 32.

SERVES 6 **HANDS-ON** 15 MINUTES **TOTAL** 30 MINUTES

1½ **pounds small turnips, peeled**
6 **tablespoons unsalted butter**
¼ **cup sorghum syrup**
2 **tablespoons (1 ounce) bourbon**
1 **tablespoon apple cider vinegar**
2 **teaspoons chopped**
    fresh rosemary
1½ **teaspoons kosher salt**
½ **teaspoon black pepper**
1 **tablespoon chopped fresh chives**

1 Halve the small turnips and quarter the large ones so all the pieces are roughly the same size. Place the turnips in a large straight-sided skillet, and add water to reach halfway up the turnips. Add 4 tablespoons of the butter, and bring to a simmer over medium. Cover, reduce the heat to low, and simmer until slightly tender, about 15 minutes.

2 Uncover and drain, reserving the cooking liquid. Return the turnips to the skillet, and stir in the sorghum, bourbon, vinegar, rosemary, salt, and 2 tablespoons of the reserved cooking liquid. Cook, stirring often, until glazed and syrupy, about 5 minutes. (If needed, you can add up to 1 additional tablespoon reserved cooking liquid to the skillet to prevent the mixture from burning and becoming too sticky.) Stir in the pepper, chives, and remaining 2 tablespoons butter; serve immediately.

Standing Rib Roast with Garlic-Porcini Rub *recipe on page 51*

HOLIDAY ROASTS

We developed and perfected 10 mouthwatering main dishes so you can pick
the pièce de résistance for your Christmas table or any grand occasion this year.

BROWN BUTTER-ROASTED BRANZINO

The nutty richness of brown butter and the bright punch of citrus and vinegar will make even the fish finicky come around after the first bite of this whole-roasted fish. Branzino is a type of sea bass with a tender, mild flesh that is delicious cooked whole for its crispy skin. It is also a fish that is high in healthy fats. Fat is a flavor carrier, and there is a lot of it in this delicious recipe.

SERVES 4 **HANDS-ON** 10 MINUTES **TOTAL** 35 MINUTES

- 2   whole branzino (about 1½ pounds), cleaned and scaled
- 2   tablespoons olive oil
- 1½ teaspoons kosher salt
- 1   teaspoon black pepper
- 6   tablespoons salted butter
- 6   fresh sage leaves
- 2   thyme sprigs
- 2   tablespoons red wine vinegar
- 2   tablespoons chopped fresh flat-leaf parsley
- 1   lemon, cut into wedges

1 Preheat the oven to 425°F. Make 3 evenly spaced ⅛-inch-deep cuts on both sides of each fish. Place a wire rack inside a rimmed baking sheet. Line the rack with a sheet of parchment paper. Coat the fish evenly with the oil. Sprinkle the outside of the fish and the inside cuts evenly with the salt and pepper. Place on the parchment-lined rack, and bake in the preheated oven until the fish flakes easily with a fork, about 25 minutes.

2 Increase the oven temperature to broil and move the oven rack to the top position. Broil the fish 5 to 6 inches from the heat until just barely charred, 3 to 4 minutes. Transfer the fish to a serving platter.

3 Combine the butter, sage, and thyme in a small skillet. Cook over medium, stirring occasionally, until the butter is browned and smells nutty, 3 to 4 minutes. Remove from heat. Remove and discard sage leaves and thyme sprigs. Stir in the vinegar. Drizzle the brown butter mixture over the fish. Sprinkle with the parsley, and serve with lemon wedges.

LEMON-THYME BISTRO CHICKEN

This is the sort of herby, lemony roast chicken that you might be served in a little hidden bistro on a cobblestone street in Aix-en-Provence (or, perhaps if you happened to be very lucky, at your grandmother's table in Tupelo). Serve this with toasty baguette slices to sop the delicious lemony pan sauce . . . unless of course you'd rather just slurp it with a straw when no one's looking.

SERVES 6 **HANDS-ON** 20 MINUTES **TOTAL** 2 HOURS, 10 MINUTES

5   tablespoons salted butter, softened
1   teaspoon black pepper
1   tablespoon lemon zest, plus 2 tablespoons fresh juice (from 1 lemon)
1½ tablespoons chopped fresh thyme
2½ teaspoons kosher salt
1   (5-pound) whole chicken
4   large garlic cloves
2   cups coarsely chopped sweet onion (about 1 medium onion)
2   cups coarsely chopped carrots (about 4 large carrots)
2   cups chopped celery (about 4 stalks)
½   cup dry white wine
¼   cup olive oil
2   tablespoons chopped fresh flat-leaf parsley
    Garnishes: kumquats, sage leaves, blood orange slices (optional)

1 Preheat the oven to 425°F. Stir together the butter, pepper, lemon zest, 1 tablespoon of the thyme, and 2 teaspoons of the salt in a small bowl.

2 Trim the excess fat from the chicken. Remove and discard the giblets, or save for another use. Pat the chicken skin very dry with paper towels. Starting at the neck of the chicken, gently loosen and lift the skin from the breasts and thighs without completely detaching it. Rub the butter mixture under the skin. Fill the chicken cavity with the garlic and 1 cup each of the onion, carrots, and celery.

3 Loosely pull the chicken legs together, and tie them with kitchen twine. Tuck the wing tips behind the chicken. Place the remaining 1 cup each onion, carrots, and celery in a rimmed baking pan. Place a wire rack over the vegetables, and place the chicken on the rack. Roast in the preheated oven 15 minutes.

4 Reduce the oven temperature to 350°F. Carefully pour the wine into the pan. (Wine will steam.) Roast until a meat thermometer inserted in the breast meat registers 160°F and the skin is golden brown, about 1 hour and 15 minutes, basting the chicken with 1 tablespoon of the oil every 15 minutes. If the chicken skin gets too dark, cover loosely with aluminum foil.

5 Remove the chicken from the oven, and let stand at least 15 minutes. Remove and discard the twine, and remove and discard the vegetables from the chicken cavity.

6 Transfer the pan vegetables and chicken to a serving platter. Pour the accumulated pan juices into a small measuring cup. Stir in the parsley, lemon juice, and remaining ½ tablespoon thyme and ½ teaspoon salt. Carve the chicken, and serve alongside the vegetables and sauce. Garnish, if desired.

FIND IT

Finding interesting garnishes for platters is often as simple as taking a trip to your local plant nursery. Wintertime is citrus season, when varieties in fruit abound. Seek out kumquat, satsuma, Key lime, and Meyer lemon trees. Clip branches with the fruit attached to tuck in around roasts (or arrange them in vases for the table). Bay laurel trees, lavender and rosemary shrubs, and potted sage in green, purple, and variegated hues provide pretty and fragrant opportunities to add interest to serving platters.

Easy Dry-Brined Roast Turkey

Seared Duck Breasts with Cherry-Port Reduction
recipe on page 46

EASY DRY-BRINED ROAST TURKEY

Order a fresh bird if possible. If frozen is a must, be sure to allow ample time (at least two days) for it to thaw thoroughly. This recipe yields a very moist, well-seasoned turkey with crisp, golden skin. The poultry seasoning blend is a perfect all-purpose mix, and the gravy that gilds the gobbler is foolproof.

SERVES 12 **HANDS-ON** 10 MINUTES **TOTAL** 28 HOURS, 10 MINUTES, INCLUDING 24 HOURS CHILLING

¼   cup kosher salt
1½ tablespoons poultry seasoning
1   tablespoon black pepper
5   tablespoons olive oil
1   (12-pound) whole fresh turkey
4   cups chicken broth
¼   cup all-purpose flour

1 Combine the salt, poultry seasoning, pepper, and 2 tablespoons of the oil in a small bowl. Remove the turkey giblets and neck; discard or reserve for another use. Pat the inside and outside of the turkey dry with paper towels. Starting at the neck, gently loosen and lift the skin from the meat without completely detaching it. Spread the salt mixture evenly under and on the skin. Cover and chill 24 to 36 hours.

2 Remove the turkey from the refrigerator; let stand at room temperature 1 hour. Loosely tie the turkey legs together with kitchen twine, and fold the wing tips back.

3 Preheat the oven to 350°F. Place the turkey, breast side up, on a wire rack in a rimmed baking pan. Drizzle the turkey evenly with the remaining 3 tablespoons oil. Place in the preheated oven; pour 2 cups of the broth into the pan. Bake until a meat thermometer inserted in the breast registers 160°F and the skin is golden brown, about 2 hours and 30 minutes, rotating the pan on the rack after 1 hour and 15 minutes. If the skin gets too dark, cover loosely with aluminum foil. Remove from the oven; let stand at least 30 minutes before carving.

4 Combine the pan drippings and 1¾ cups of the broth in a small saucepan; bring to a boil over medium-high. Reduce the heat to medium, and cook, stirring occasionally, until reduced to about 2 cups. Whisk together the flour and remaining ¼ cup of the broth in a bowl until smooth. Add the flour mixture to the drippings; bring to a boil, and cook until thickened, about 1 minute.

5 Carve the turkey, and serve with the gravy.

SEARED DUCK BREASTS WITH CHERRY-PORT REDUCTION

Start preparing the duck, skin side down, in a cold pan to slowly render the fat and ensure extra-crispy skin. By the end of cooking, you will have about a half cup duck fat. In the South, we may love our bacon grease, but duck fat is a top chef's liquid gold! A potato cooked in duck fat will make your knees buckle, but eat too many and you may need to loosen your belt buckle. This pan sauce comes together fast; no need to stir it constantly. Do monitor the duck closely. It will overcook and dry out quickly. Photo page 44.

SERVES 4 **HANDS-ON** 15 MINUTES **TOTAL** 25 MINUTES

4 (7-ounce) boneless, skin-on duck breasts
1 teaspoon kosher salt
½ teaspoon black pepper
½ cup port
⅓ cup dried cherries
2 tablespoons light brown sugar
⅓ cup golden raisins
3 tablespoons chopped fresh flat-leaf parsley
2 tablespoons red wine vinegar

1 Using a sharp knife, cut through the duck skin in parallel lines, being careful not to cut all the way through the meat. Turn the breasts 45°, and cut through the skin in parallel lines perpendicular to the first set of lines, creating a crosshatch pattern. Sprinkle the duck breasts evenly with ¾ teaspoon of the salt and ¼ teaspoon of the pepper. Place the duck breasts, skin sides down, in a large, room-temperature skillet. Place on the stove top, and heat over medium-high. Cook until the duck skin is golden brown, 8 to 10 minutes.

2 Turn the duck breasts, and cook until a meat thermometer inserted in the thickest portion of the duck registers 120°F, 2 to 3 minutes. Remove from the skillet. Let stand at least 10 minutes before slicing.

3 Reserve 1 tablespoon pan drippings in the skillet, and discard the remaining drippings. Add the port, cherries, brown sugar, and remaining ¼ teaspoon each salt and pepper to skillet. Bring to a boil over medium-high. Reduce the heat to medium-low, and simmer until mixture is slightly thickened, 4 to 5 minutes. Remove from the heat, and stir in the raisins, parsley, and red wine vinegar.

4 Slice the duck, and serve with the cherry-port reduction.

MUSTARD, GARLIC, AND SAGE PORK CROWN ROAST

This is such an impressive golden-brown roast with rich, complex flavors. Have your local butcher cut the pork and tie it for you to take some of the prep off your busy holiday plate.
Photo page 49.

SERVES 12 **HANDS-ON** 15 MINUTES **TOTAL** 3 HOURS

¼ cup olive oil

3 tablespoons Dijon mustard

3 tablespoons finely chopped garlic (about 12 cloves)

3 tablespoons finely chopped fresh sage

1½ tablespoons kosher salt

2 teaspoons black pepper

2 (4-pound) bone-in pork rib roasts (about 6 bones each), frenched

1½ cups water

1 Preheat the oven to 250°F. Process the oil, mustard, garlic, sage, salt, and pepper in a food processor until smooth.

2 Place the pork loins beside each other on a work surface with the tips of the bones pointing up and the meaty sides facing out. Curve the racks toward each other so both ends meet to form a circle, cutting the pork as necessary to curve the racks. Tie kitchen twine around the meaty parts of the pork loins, tightly securing the circle in place. Spread the mustard mixture evenly over the pork.

3 Place the pork on a wire rack in a roasting pan. Place in the preheated oven, and pour the water into the pan. Roast until a meat thermometer inserted in the thickest portion registers 135°F, about 2 hours. Remove from the oven, and let stand 15 minutes. Increase the oven temperature to 500°F. Return the pork to the oven, and roast until the outside is browned, about 10 minutes. Remove from the oven, and let stand 20 minutes before cutting into chops.

BACON-WRAPPED PORK LOIN WITH CRANBERRY-APPLE GLAZE

Crisp bacon in both the sauce and the wrap adds a smoky richness to a very lean pork tenderloin.
Cranberries add tang and a touch of holiday color to the sweet glaze.

SERVES 8 **HANDS-ON** 20 MINUTES **TOTAL** 1 HOUR, 15 MINUTES

14 thick-cut bacon slices
1 (3-pound) pork tenderloin
1 teaspoon kosher salt
1 teaspoon black pepper
½ cup fresh cranberries (about 3 ounces)
⅓ cup apple jelly
⅓ cup water
2 tablespoons apple cider vinegar

1 Preheat the oven to 400°F. Chop 6 of the bacon slices. Place the chopped bacon in a large cast-iron skillet, and heat over medium-high. Cook the bacon until crispy, about 8 minutes. Using a slotted spoon, remove the bacon from the skillet, and place on a plate lined with paper towels to drain, reserving the drippings in the skillet.

2 Sprinkle the pork with ¾ teaspoon each of the salt and pepper. Place the pork in the skillet; cook over medium-high, turning to brown on all sides, about 6 minutes. Remove the pork from the skillet, and wrap remaining 8 bacon slices around the pork. Place a wire rack inside a rimmed baking sheet, and place the bacon-wrapped pork on the rack. Roast in the preheated oven until the bacon is done and a meat thermometer inserted in the thickest portion of the pork registers 135°F, 35 to 40 minutes. Remove the pork from the skillet, reserving the drippings in the skillet. Let the pork stand at least 15 minutes before slicing.

3 Prepare the Cranberry-Apple Glaze: Heat the skillet over medium. Add the chopped bacon, cranberries, jelly, water, vinegar, and remaining ¼ teaspoon each salt and pepper. Bring to a boil, and cook, stirring occasionally, until the cranberries have burst and mixture is slightly thickened, about 3 minutes.

4 Cut the pork into 2½-inch-thick slices, and top the servings with the Cranberry-Apple Glaze.

Mustard, Garlic, and Sage Pork Crown Roast
recipe on page 47

Bacon-Wrapped Pork Loin with Cranberry-Apple Glaze

ROAST BEEF TENDERLOIN WITH CREMINI-MADEIRA SAUCE

This is an elegant, melt-in-your-mouth main course. There are a few tricks to perfecting it. You will have to curve the loin to fit it in the skillet. It's crucial to get the pan hot again before adding the mushrooms; otherwise they will steam instead of sear. You want them to brown a bit. Also be sure to stir the butter into the sauce completely at the end to ensure the fat doesn't separate in the sauce. Photo page 52.

SERVES 12 **HANDS-ON** 25 MINUTES **TOTAL** 1 HOUR

1   (4-pound) beef tenderloin, trimmed and trussed
1½ teaspoons kosher salt
1   teaspoon black pepper
2   tablespoons canola oil
6   tablespoons salted butter
1   pound cremini mushrooms, quartered
¼   cup finely chopped shallot (about 1 large shallot)
1   tablespoon finely chopped garlic (about 4 cloves)
1   cup Madeira
3   tablespoons chopped fresh flat-leaf parsley
2   tablespoons heavy cream
    Garnishes: rosemary sprigs, pomegranate wedges (optional)

1   Preheat the oven to 425°F. Sprinkle the beef with 1 teaspoon of the salt and ¾ teaspoon of the pepper. Heat the oil in a large ovenproof skillet over medium-high. Place the beef in the skillet; cook, turning to brown on all sides, 8 to 10 minutes.

2   Transfer the skillet to the preheated oven, and roast until a meat thermometer inserted in the thickest portion registers 130°F, 30 to 40 minutes. Remove the beef from the skillet, reserving the drippings in the skillet. Let stand at least 10 minutes before slicing. Remove and discard the twine.

3   Heat the skillet over medium-high. Add 3 tablespoons of the butter, and cook until melted. Add the mushrooms; cook, stirring occasionally, until well browned, about 8 minutes. Add the shallot and garlic; cook, stirring occasionally, until tender, about 3 minutes. Add the Madeira, and bring to a boil. Reduce the heat to medium-low, and simmer until the liquid is reduced by about half and slightly thickened, about 5 minutes. Remove from the heat, and stir in the parsley, cream, and remaining 3 tablespoons butter, ½ teaspoon salt, and ¼ teaspoon pepper.

4   Slice the beef, and serve with the Cremini-Madeira Sauce. Garnish, if desired.

STANDING RIB ROAST WITH GARLIC-PORCINI RUB

A standing rib roast is the same as a prime rib roast and is an impressive "company's coming" cut for the holiday table. Order the roast from your butcher a week or two before you are ready to pick it up; ask for it to be "frenched" or trimmed for you. Photo page 38.

SERVES 8 **HANDS-ON** 20 MINUTES **TOTAL** 2 HOURS, 10 MINUTES

12 garlic cloves
½ ounce dried porcini mushrooms
2 teaspoons kosher salt
1½ teaspoons black pepper
3 tablespoons olive oil
1 tablespoon whole-grain mustard
1 (5-pound) bone-in standing rib roast, frenched
1 cup water

1 Preheat the oven to 325°F. Process the garlic, mushrooms, salt, and pepper in a miniature food processor until very finely chopped. Add the oil and mustard; process until well combined.

2 Place the roast on a wire rack coated with cooking spray in a rimmed baking pan. Rub the garlic mixture evenly over the roast. Place in the preheated oven, and pour the water in the baking pan. Roast until a meat thermometer inserted in the thickest portion registers 110°F, about 1 hour and 30 minutes. If the beef starts to become too dark, cover loosely with aluminum foil.

3 Remove from the oven, and discard the pan drippings. Increase the oven temperature to 500°F. Return the beef to the oven, and roast until well browned, 5 to 10 minutes.

4 Remove from the oven, and let stand at least 15 minutes before slicing.

Roast Beef Tenderloin with Cremini-Madeira Sauce
recipe on page 50

Pistachio- and Parmesan-Crusted Lamb Rack
recipe on page 54

Herb-Marinated Leg of Lamb
recipe on page 55

PISTACHIO- AND PARMESAN-CRUSTED LAMB RACK

A crunchy coating of pistachios and breadcrumbs complements tender lamb. Parmesan and garlic harmonize with the pronounced flavors of the meat. Photo page 53.

SERVES 4 **HANDS-ON** 15 MINUTES **TOTAL** 50 MINUTES

½   cup shelled pistachios
2   ounces Parmesan cheese, grated (about ½ cup)
2   ounces baguette, torn into small pieces
2   garlic cloves
3   tablespoons olive oil
2   (1-pound) racks of lamb, frenched
1¼   teaspoons kosher salt
½   teaspoon black pepper
¼   cup Dijon mustard

1 Preheat the oven to 450°F. Process the pistachios, Parmesan, baguette, and garlic in a food processor until finely ground. Add the oil; pulse until just combined.

2 Pat the racks of lamb dry with paper towels. Sprinkle evenly with the salt and pepper, and rub the mustard over the lamb. Sprinkle the pistachio mixture over the lamb, pressing to adhere. Place the racks of lamb on a roasting rack coated with cooking spray. Place the roasting rack inside a roasting pan. Roast in the preheated oven 10 minutes.

3 Without removing the lamb from the oven, reduce the oven temperature to 400°F. Roast until a meat thermometer inserted in the thickest portion registers 125°F (for medium-rare), about 12 minutes. Remove from the oven, and let stand 10 minutes before cutting into chops.

HERB-MARINATED LEG OF LAMB

Your guests will appreciate the bold, bright flavors that come from the lemon-and-herb marinade on this broiled lamb. The charred exterior adds another complex flavor layer. Photo page 53.

SERVES 8 HANDS-ON 20 MINUTES TOTAL 13 HOURS, 25 MINUTES, INCLUDING 12 HOURS MARINATING

1   cup chopped fresh flat-leaf parsley stems
6   garlic cloves
1   tablespoon kosher salt
½   teaspoon black pepper
1½ cups packed fresh mint leaves
¾   cup, plus 2 tablespoons extra-virgin olive oil
2   tablespoons lemon zest, plus ½ cup and 1 tablespoon fresh juice (from 5 lemons)
1   (3-pound) boneless leg of lamb, butterflied to 2-inch thickness
1   tablespoon chopped fresh rosemary
½   cup packed fresh flat-leaf parsley leaves
    Garnishes: round lime slices, mint leaves, and parsley leaves (optional)

1 Process the parsley stems, garlic, salt, pepper, 1 cup of the mint, ½ cup of the oil, and 1 tablespoon of the lemon juice in a blender until smooth. Place the lamb in a large resealable plastic freezer bag. Add the herb mixture; massage to coat the lamb evenly. Seal the bag, and chill 12 to 24 hours.

2 Remove the lamb from the bag, and discard the marinade. Place the lamb on a rimmed baking sheet. Sprinkle evenly with the rosemary. Cover and let stand at room temperature 1 hour.

3 Preheat the broiler to high with the oven rack 8 inches from the heat. Broil the lamb until the top is charred, 12 to 16 minutes. Turn the lamb, and broil until a meat thermometer inserted in thickest portion registers 125°F (for medium-rare), 10 to 12 minutes. Remove from the oven, and let stand 10 minutes before slicing.

4 Chop the remaining ½ cup mint leaves, and place in a small bowl with the parsley leaves, lemon zest, and remaining 6 tablespoons oil and ½ cup lemon juice. Stir to combine.

5 Slice the lamb, and serve with the mint mixture. Garnish, if desired.

HOLIDAY DESSERTS

'Tis the season, and if ever you needed a reason to indulge,
we have the cakes, bread, cookies, and cheesecake to make it easy.

STUMP DE NOËL

We've taken the classic bûche de Noël and flipped it upright for a whole new perspective. Store-bought meringue mushrooms, pistachios, and sliced almonds combine to create a mossy woodland effect.

SERVES 12 **HANDS-ON** 1 HOUR, 5 MINUTES **TOTAL** 2 HOURS, 40 MINUTES

6   ounces bittersweet baking chocolate, finely chopped
1   cup salted butter, softened
2   cups granulated sugar
3   large eggs
1   tablespoon vanilla extract
2¾ cups unbleached cake flour
¼   cup unsweetened cocoa
1   teaspoon baking powder
½   teaspoon table salt
½   teaspoon baking soda
2   cups whole buttermilk
    Chocolate-Coffee Buttercream
    Chocolate Fudge Buttercream
    Powdered sugar

1 Preheat the oven to 350°F. Grease and flour 3 9-inch round cake pans.

2 Microwave the chocolate in a microwavable bowl on MEDIUM (50% power) until smooth, 1 minute. Beat the butter with a heavy-duty electric stand mixer on medium until creamy; beat in the sugar until fluffy. Add the eggs, 1 at a time, beating after each addition. Add the chocolate and vanilla, beating at low just until blended.

3 Sift the cake flour and the next 4 ingredients in a medium bowl. Add the flour mixture to the butter mixture alternately with the buttermilk, beating on low just until blended after each addition. Divide the batter among the prepared pans.

4 Bake in the preheated oven until a wooden pick inserted in the center comes out clean, about 25 minutes. Cool in the pans on wire racks 10 minutes; remove from pans to wire racks to cool completely, about 1 hour.

5 Place 1 cake layer on a plate; frost the top with ½ cup Chocolate-Coffee Buttercream; top with the second cake layer; frost top with ½ cup more of the Chocolate-Coffee Buttercream.

6 Top with the last cake layer. Frost the sides with the Chocolate Fudge Buttercream, raking upward with the tines of a fork to resemble bark. Continue to frost the top with a thin layer. Spread a thin layer of the Chocolate-Coffee Buttercream on top of the Chocolate Fudge Buttercream, spreading to edge of cake.

7 Using the tines of a fork, make circular patterns in the buttercream so some darker Chocolate Fudge Buttercream shows through to resemble tree rings. Using a small offset spatula, rake a small amount of Chocolate-Coffee Buttercream in an upward motion on the sides of the cake. Dust the top lightly with powdered sugar.

Chocolate-Coffee Buttercream: Microwave ¼ cup whipping cream in a microwavable bowl on MEDIUM (50% power) until warm, 45 seconds. Add 1 tablespoon instant coffee granules. Stir until dissolved; cool 10 minutes. Beat ⅔ cup softened salted butter with an electric mixer on medium speed until smooth. Whisk together 2½ cups powdered sugar and 1 tablespoon unsweetened cocoa in a small bowl. Gradually add powdered sugar mixture alternately with 1 tesapoon vanilla extract and cream mixture, beating until smooth, about 2 minutes.

Chocolate-Fudge Buttercream: Microwave 2 ounces finely chopped bittersweet baking chocolate in a small microwaveable bowl at MEDIUM (50% power) until melted, 45 seconds, stirring every 15 seconds. Let stand 10 minutes. Beat 1 cup softened salted butter with an electric mixer on medium speed until creamy. Whisk together 6 cups powdered sugar and ⅓ cup unsweetened cocoa, and gradually add to butter alternately with ½ cup whipping cream, beating on low speed until combined. Add the melted chocolate; increase speed to medium, and beat until light and fluffy, 3 to 4 minutes.

PANETTONE

This domed sweet loaf, studded with fruit, is a holiday favorite in Italy. It has a much more tender crumb and buttery flavor than Grandma's boozy fruitcake. It makes a pretty gift too. If you can't find the tall traditional panettone mold, you can make your own by using clean, empty coffee cans.

SERVES 20 **HANDS-ON** 1 HOUR, 55 MINUTES **TOTAL** 8 HOURS, INCLUDING 2 HOURS COOLING

1 cup golden raisins

½ cup dried cherries

⅓ cup (2⅔ ounces) orange liqueur

2 (¼-ounce) envelopes active dry yeast

1 cup warm whole milk (105°F to 115°F)

1 cup all-purpose flour

4 cups bread flour

¾ cup granulated sugar

4 large egg yolks

2 large eggs

2 teaspoons vanilla extract

2 teaspoons kosher salt

12 tablespoons unsalted butter, softened

½ cup chopped roasted unsalted pistachios

1 Combine the raisins, cherries, and orange liqueur in a small bowl; let the fruit stand until ready to use, stirring occasionally.

2 Sprinkle the yeast over the warm milk in a medium bowl. Let stand until foamy, about 5 minutes. Add the all-purpose flour, 1 cup of the bread flour, and 2 tablespoons of the sugar, and stir until the mixture forms a thick, smooth paste. Cover the bowl with plastic wrap, and let stand in a warm place (80°F to 85°F), free from drafts, 1 hour and 30 minutes. (This mixture is called a sponge.)

3 Combine the yolks, eggs, vanilla, salt, and remaining sugar in the bowl of a heavy-duty electric stand mixer fitted with a paddle attachment; beat on low speed until combined. Add the sponge; beat on low speed until combined.

4 Change the paddle to the dough hook. Add the remaining 3 cups bread flour; beat mixture on medium-low speed until dough is smooth and elastic, 10 to 12 minutes. Increase speed to medium, and beat until dough begins to form a ball and pulls away from sides of bowl, about 5 minutes. Reduce mixer to low speed; add 10 tablespoons of the butter, 1 tablespoon at a time, beating until combined after each addition. Increase speed to medium-high and beat until smooth and elastic, about 5 minutes. Reduce speed to low; add raisin mixture and pistachios. Beat at low speed until combined.

5 Transfer the dough to a large lightly greased (with cooking spray) bowl. Cover with plastic wrap, and let stand in a warm place (80°F to 85°F), free from drafts, 1 hour and 30 minutes. Fold dough in half 2 times in bowl; cover, and let stand 15 minutes.

6 Place the dough on a lightly floured surface. Divide dough in half. Form each half into a ball; place each ball into a 5¼×3¾-inch disposable panettone mold (these can be found at Sur La Table) or 2 (13-ounce) clean coffee cans, lightly greased (with cooking spray). Transfer to doubled (2 stacked) baking sheets; cover with plastic wrap, and let stand in a warm place (80°F to 85°F), free from drafts, until doubled in size, about 1 hour.

7 Preheat oven to 350°F. Melt remaining 2 tablespoons butter; brush top of each panettone dough with about half of the butter; reserve remaining butter. Bake in preheated oven on doubled baking sheets until tops are deep brown and a knife inserted in centers comes out clean, 50 to 55 minutes. Remove from oven, and brush tops of panettone with reserved melted butter. Remove from pans, and place loaves on wire rack; cool completely before slicing, about 2 hours.

Christmas Tree Mini Cakes
recipe on page 65

Mini Meringue Christmas Wreaths
recipe on page 64

MINI MERINGUE CHRISTMAS WREATHS

Get out the piping tips and have some fun! Meringues are so delicate and pretty . . . and forgiving too. Make a mistake? Turn it into a snowman. This recipe is for French-style meringue stabilized with cream of tartar. Photo page 63.

SERVES 10 **HANDS-ON** 35 MINUTES **TOTAL** 4 HOURS, 35 MINUTES

1 tablespoon cornstarch
1 cup, plus 3 tablespoons granulated sugar
4 large egg whites, at room temperature
¼ teaspoon cream of tartar
⅛ teaspoon table salt
1½ teaspoons vanilla extract
1 cup heavy cream
   Assorted sliced and whole fresh berries (blueberries, raspberries, blackberries, and strawberries)
   Mint leaves

1 Preheat the oven to 225°F. Stir together the cornstarch and 1 cup of the sugar in a small bowl.

2 Beat the egg whites with a heavy-duty stand mixer on medium-high speed until foamy; add the cream of tartar and salt, beating until blended, about 1 minute. Gradually add the sugar mixture, 1 tablespoon at a time, beating well after each addition on medium-high speed until the mixture is glossy, stiff peaks form, and sugar dissolves. (Do not overbeat, but the meringue should be smooth without any granules.) Beat in 1 teaspoon of the vanilla just until blended.

3 Draw 10 (4-inch) circles onto 2 baking sheets lined with parchment paper; turn the paper over. Gently spread or pipe the meringue into 2-inch-tall × 2-inch-wide rings on paper, using the circles as a guide. Bake in the preheated oven 1 hour and 30 minutes. Turn the oven off; let the meringues stand in the closed oven until completely dry, at least 2 hours. Carefully remove the meringues from the paper.

4 Beat the heavy cream with a heavy-duty stand mixer fitted with the whisk attachment on medium-high speed until foamy; gradually beat in the remaining 3 tablespoons sugar and ½ teaspoon vanilla until medium peaks form. Dollop or pipe the whipped cream on top of the meringues. Decoratively place the berries on the wreaths; add mint leaves for garnish.

MERINGUE MASTERY

Meringue is a combination of beaten egg whites and sugar. Cream of tartar, an acid, may be added as a stabilizer, sugar to sweeten, and extracts to flavor. Three general styles of meringue are referred to in baking:

Italian Meringue: A stable, glossy meringue made by slowly beating hot sugar syrup into soft egg white peaks that are then beaten to firm, shiny peaks. Italian meringue is used to stabilize buttercream and lighten mousse.

Swiss Meringue: Room-temperature egg whites with no trace of fat, along with sugar and cream of tartar, are heated in a double boiler, and then whipped into clouds. Swiss meringue makes crisp meringue cake layers.

French Meringue: Stiff, sweetened peaks of raw egg whites are cooked after being whipped to billowy heights—either on their own, on top of pies, or folded into soufflés.

CHRISTMAS TREE MINI CAKES

Set a table just for the kiddos to get creative and let them have artistic fun with the cookie decorations! Or, if that kind of mess is more than you bargained for, invite your friends instead. It's much more fun to catch up while getting craftsy together and checking a few holiday to-dos off your gift list for teachers, colleagues, coaches, and neighbors. Photo page 63.

SERVES 20 **HANDS-ON** 20 MINUTES **TOTAL** 9 HOURS, 15 MINUTES, INCLUDING 8 HOURS CHILLING

1½ cups salted butter, softened
1 (8-ounce) package cream cheese, softened
3 cups granulated sugar
6 large eggs
3 cups all-purpose flour
½ teaspoon baking powder
¼ teaspoon table salt
1½ teaspoons vanilla extract
½ teaspoon almond extract
Vanilla Buttercream
Assorted sprinkles, dragées, and sugar pearls

1 Preheat the oven to 325°F. Beat the butter and cream cheese with a heavy-duty stand mixer on medium speed until creamy; gradually add the sugar, and beat until light and fluffy. Add the eggs, 1 at a time, beating until just combined after each addition.

2 Stir together the flour, baking powder, and salt in a bowl; gradually add to the butter mixture, beating until combined. Stir in the vanilla and almond extracts. Pour the batter into a generously greased and floured 17×12-inch rimmed baking sheet lined with parchment paper (leaving 3 extra inches on each end to use as handles to lift the cake out of the pan); lightly grease (with cooking spray) parchment paper.

3 Bake in the preheated oven until a wooden pick inserted in the center comes out clean, 30 to 35 minutes. Cool in the pan on a wire rack, 10 minutes. Carefully lift the cake out of the pan using the parchment paper handles, and cool completely on a wire rack, about 1 hour. Wrap in plastic wrap, and chill 8 hours or overnight.

4 On a sheet of parchment or cardboard, draw a 3-inch straight-sided Christmas tree; cut out and use as a stencil to cut trees out of chilled cake. Frost with Vanilla Buttercream, and decorate as desired.

Vanilla Buttercream: Beat ¾ cup softened salted butter, 1 tablespoon vanilla extract, and ¼ teaspoon table salt with an electric mixer on medium speed until creamy. Gradually add 6 cups powdered sugar alternately with 6 tablespoons milk, 1 tablespoon at time, beating on low speed until blended and smooth after each addition. Beat in up to 2 tablespoons additional milk, if needed, for desired consistency.

GINGER STAR NAPOLEONS WITH FLUFFY GINGER CREAM

Twinkle, twinkle! It's amazing how a stack of humble sugar cookies is transformed into a three-star restaurant-caliber dessert with a few layers of flavored whipped cream nestled in between. This showstopper finale is light, elegant, and beyond simple to pull together.

SERVES 4 **HANDS-ON** 30 MINUTES **TOTAL** 2 HOURS, 30 MINUTES

2   **cups all-purpose flour**
1½ **teaspoons ground ginger**
½   **teaspoon table salt**
1   **cup salted butter, softened**
½   **cup powdered sugar**
1   **tablespoon grated fresh ginger**
½   **teaspoon vanilla extract**
2   **tablespoons heavy cream**
1   **large egg**
¼   **cup coarse sparkling sugar**
   Fluffy Ginger Cream
8   **teaspoons finely chopped crystallized ginger**
   Garnishes: fresh cranberries, fresh thyme sprigs (optional)

1 Whisk together the flour, ground ginger, and salt in a medium bowl until combined.

2 Beat the butter in a large bowl with an electric mixer on medium speed until creamy; gradually add the powdered sugar, beating until combined after each addition. Beat in the grated ginger and vanilla. Gradually add the flour mixture; beat just until blended.

3 Divide the dough in half, and flatten each half into a disk. Wrap each disk in plastic wrap, and chill until firm, about 1 hour and 30 minutes.

4 Preheat the oven to 350°F. Line 2 large baking sheets with parchment paper. Roll out dough, 1 disk at a time, to ¼-inch thickness on a lightly floured surface. Cut into star shapes, using a 4-inch cookie cutter. Place ½ inch apart on prepared baking sheets. (You should have 16 cookies total.)

5 Whisk together the heavy cream and egg in a small bowl, and brush the egg wash lightly over the cookies. Sprinkle generously with the sparkling sugar.

6 Bake in the preheated oven until the cookies are golden brown around edges, 11 to 12 minutes. Cool on the baking sheets 2 minutes; remove with the parchment paper to wire racks to cool completely, 20 minutes.

7 To assemble the Napoleons: Place 1 cookie on a serving plate, and dollop with about 2 tablespoons of the Fluffy Ginger Cream. Top with a second cookie, and dollop with about 2 tablespoons Ginger Cream. Top with a third cookie, and dollop with about 2 tablespoons Ginger Cream. Sprinkle 2 teaspoons crystallized ginger on top of each Napoleon. Garnish, if desired.

Fluffy Ginger Cream: Beat 1 cup heavy cream, 3 tablespoons powdered sugar, and 1 teaspoon vanilla extract with an electric stand mixer fitted with the whisk attachment on medium-high speed until stiff peaks form, 2 to 3 minutes. Add 2 tablespoons ginger liqueur; beat until well combined, about 1 minute.

OLD-FASHIONED EGGNOG CHEESECAKE

*There are countless combinations to be
exalted: peanut butter and chocolate, tacos
and Tuesday, moonshine and Mason jars,
but you haven't swooned until you've tried
a forkful of eggnog-meets-cheesecake.
Promise!*

SERVES 8 **HANDS-ON** 20 MINUTES **TOTAL** 9 HOURS, 20 MINUTES,
INCLUDING 8 HOURS CHILLING

2	cups finely crushed Biscoff cookies
¼	cup granulated sugar
¼	cup salted butter, melted
4	(8-ounce) packages cream cheese, softened
4	large eggs
¼	cup (2 ounces) dark rum
1½	cups refrigerated eggnog
2	cups powdered sugar
2	tablespoons all-purpose flour
⅛	teaspoon table salt
1	cup heavy cream
	Freshly grated nutmeg (optional)

1 Preheat oven to 350°F. Stir together the ground cookies,
granulated sugar, and butter in a medium bowl; press
mixture onto bottom and up sides of a 10-inch springform
pan. Bake in the preheated oven 8 minutes. Cool on a wire
rack until ready to use.

2 Reduce the oven temperature to 325°F. Beat the cream
cheese with a heavy-duty stand mixer on medium speed
until smooth; add the eggs, 1 at a time, beating just until
blended after each addition. Add the rum and 1¼ cups
of the eggnog; beat until blended. Stir together the
powdered sugar, flour, and salt in a small bowl; gently fold
the powdered sugar mixture into the cream cheese mixture
until blended. Pour the mixture into the cooled crust.

3 Bake at 325°F until the center jiggles slightly when touched,
1 hour. Turn off the oven and leave cheesecake inside with
the oven door open 10 minutes. Transfer to a wire rack.
Run a knife between the cheesecake and pan rim; let cool
completely. Cover and chill 8 hours.

4 Beat the heavy cream and remaining ¼ cup eggnog with
an electric mixer on medium-high speed until stiff peaks
form. Remove sides of pan, and place cheesecake on a
serving plate. Gently blot any moisture that has collected
on top of cheesecake with a paper towel. Dollop or spread
whipped cream mixture over top of cheesecake, and, if
desired, sprinkle with freshly grated nutmeg.

Coconut Layer Cake
recipe on page 97

HOLIDAY
WHITE CAKES

There's perhaps no cake in the South quite as important as the cake served on the holiday table. In 1995, *Southern Living* magazine featured a photograph of a three-layer Coconut-Lemon Cake on the cover. The overwhelming reader response to this cake began a tradition of "the big white cake," as the staff calls it, adorning the cover every December.

PEPPERMINT CAKE WITH SEVEN-MINUTE FROSTING

Cool peppermint-vanilla cake and fluffy pink buttercream make a merry combination. Finish with whimsical dollops of mint frosting. The cake layers and buttercream can be made ahead to save time.

SERVES 12 **HANDS-ON** 1 HOUR, 20 MINUTES **TOTAL** 2 HOURS, 40 MINUTES

CAKE LAYERS

- 2 cups granulated sugar
- 1¼ cups unsalted butter, softened
- 4 large eggs
- 2 tablespoons vanilla extract
- 4 cups unbleached cake flour
- 1 tablespoon baking powder
- ½ teaspoon baking soda
- ½ teaspoon table salt
- 1 cup whole milk
  Shortening, for greasing pans

PEPPERMINT BUTTERCREAM

- 3 cups powdered sugar
- 1 cup unsalted butter, softened
- ½ cup finely crushed hard peppermint candies (about 20 candies)
- 1 teaspoon vanilla extract
- ½ teaspoon table salt
- 1 to 2 teaspoons whole milk
- 2 to 3 drops liquid red food coloring

SEVEN-MINUTE FROSTING

- 12 large egg whites
- 3 cups granulated sugar
- 3 tablespoons corn syrup
- 1 teaspoon table salt
- ½ teaspoon peppermint extract

FOR DECORATING

- 1¼ cups hard peppermint candies
- 1¼ teaspoons white Disco Dust

1 Prepare the Cake Layers: Preheat the oven to 350°F. Beat the granulated sugar and butter with an electric mixer on medium speed until light and fluffy, about 2 minutes. Add eggs, 1 at a time, and beat just until combined after each addition. Add vanilla, and beat just until combined. Whisk together flour, baking powder, baking soda, and salt in a medium bowl. Add flour mixture, in batches, alternately with milk, beginning and ending with flour mixture. Beat on low speed just until blended after each addition. Pour batter into 2 greased (with shortening) and floured 9-inch round cake pans.

2 Bake in the preheated oven until a wooden pick inserted in centers comes out clean, 28 to 30 minutes. Cool in pans on wire racks 20 minutes; remove from pans to wire racks, and cool completely, about 30 minutes.

3 Prepare the Peppermint Buttercream: Beat powdered sugar and butter with an electric mixer on medium speed until smooth, about 2 minutes. Add crushed peppermints, vanilla, and salt; beat until blended. Beat in 1 teaspoon of the milk. Beat in up to 1 more teaspoon of milk, ¼ teaspoon at a time, until desired consistency is reached. Beat in food coloring, 1 drop at a time, until desired color is reached.

4 Prepare the Seven-Minute Frosting: Pour water to a depth of 2 inches into bottom of a saucepan or double boiler; bring to a simmer over medium heat. Stir together egg whites, granulated sugar, corn syrup, and salt in a heatproof bowl or top of double boiler. Place bowl over simmering water, and whisk constantly until sugar dissolves and mixture is hot, about 7 minutes. Remove from heat, and beat with an electric mixer on medium-high speed until stiff peaks form and mixture is completely cooled, about 10 minutes. Beat in peppermint extract.

5 Assemble the Cake: Place 1 Cake Layer on a cake plate. Spread Peppermint Buttercream in an even layer, about ½ inch thick, to within ½ inch of cake edge. Top with remaining Cake Layer.

6 Decorate the Cake: Spread enough of the cooled frosting over top and sides of cake to cover.

7 Roughly crush 1 cup of the peppermint candies into small pieces. Crush the remaining ¼ cup candies into fine pieces; set aside. Add 1 teaspoon of the Disco Dust to the 1 cup crushed candy; stir to combine.

8 Spoon the remaining Frosting into a resealable plastic bag, and snip corner of the bag. Pipe swirls of Frosting on top of the cake. Lightly press the Disco Dust-coated crushed candy into the sides of the frosted cake until the sides are coated. Sprinkle the piped swirls with the finely crushed candy and an additional ½ teaspoon Disco Dust.

PUMPKIN TIRAMISU CAKE

The "tiramisu" flavor in this fancy cake comes from Coffee Syrup that soaks into it and Maple Mascarpone Cream between its layers.

SERVES 12 **HANDS-ON** 1 HOUR **TOTAL** 2 HOURS, 45 MINUTES

CAKE LAYERS

- 3 eggs, at room temperature
  Shortening
- ¾ cup all-purpose flour
- 2 teaspoons ground cinnamon
- 1 teaspoon baking powder
- 1 teaspoon ground ginger
- ½ teaspoon table salt
- ½ teaspoon ground nutmeg
- 1 cup granulated sugar
- ⅔ cup canned pumpkin
- 1 teaspoon lemon juice
- 1 cup finely chopped hazelnuts
  Powdered sugar

COFFEE SYRUP

- ½ cup granulated sugar
- ½ cup water
- 2 tablespoons instant espresso coffee powder
- 1 tablespoon Amaretto
- 1 tablespoon hazelnut liqueur

MAPLE MASCARPONE CREAM

- 2 cups whipping cream
- 1 (8-ounce) container mascarpone cheese
- ¼ cup pure maple syrup

GARNISHES

Chopped toasted hazelnuts (optional)
Grated bittersweet chocolate (optional)

1 Prepare the Cake: Lightly grease (with shortening) 1 (15×10-inch) baking pan. Line the bottom of the pan with waxed paper; grease the paper. In a small bowl stir together the flour, cinnamon, baking powder, ginger, salt, and nutmeg; set aside.

2 Preheat the oven to 375°F. In a large mixing bowl beat eggs with a stand mixer on high speed 5 minutes or until thick and lemon color. Gradually add the sugar, beating on medium speed until fluffy. Stir in the pumpkin and lemon juice. Add the flour mixture, and beat on low speed just until combined. Pour the batter into the pan, spreading evenly. Sprinkle with nuts.

3 Bake in preheated oven 15 minutes or until cake springs back when lightly touched. Immediately loosen edges of cake from pan, and turn cake out onto a towel sprinkled with powdered sugar. Remove waxed paper, and cool completely on a wire rack, (about 30 minutes).

4 Prepare the Coffee Syrup: In a small saucepan combine the sugar, water, and instant espresso coffee powder. Bring to boiling over medium, stirring to dissolve sugar. Boil gently 1 minute. Remove from heat. Stir in Amaretto and hazelnut liqueur.

5 Prepare the Maple Mascarpone Cream: In a large mixing bowl beat whipping cream, mascarpone cheese, and maple syrup with an electric mixer on medium to high speed until soft peaks form (the tips curl).

6 Assemble the Cake: Cut the cake crosswise into thirds. Place one of the cake layers nuts side up on a serving plate. Drizzle one-third of the Coffee Syrup over Cake Layer. Spread evenly with ¾ cup Maple Mascarpone Cream. Repeat the layers. Top with the remaining Cake Layer, and drizzle with remaining Coffee Syrup. Frost the top and sides of the cake with the remaining Maple Mascarpone Cream.

7 Cover the cake, and chill 2 to 24 hours. If desired, garnish the top of the cake with additional chopped hazelnuts and grated bittersweet chocolate.

Note: To toast hazelnuts, spread them in a single layer on a rimmed baking sheet. Bake in a 350°F oven 7 to 9 minutes, stirring once, until golden and the skins start to split. When the nuts have cooled slightly, put them on a clean kitchen towel, and rub vigorously to remove as much of the skins as you can.

SPICE CAKE WITH CRANBERRY FILLING

A creamy Apple Cider Frosting adds to the holiday flavors of warm spices and sweet-tart cranberry in this impressive cake.

SERVES 10 TO 12 **HANDS-ON** 1 HOUR, 15 MINUTES **TOTAL** 11 HOURS, 15 MINUTES, INCLUDING 8 HOURS CHILLING

CRANBERRY FILLING

2	cups fresh or frozen whole cranberries
1	cup granulated sugar
3	tablespoons fresh orange juice
2	tablespoons cornstarch
1	tablespoon cold water
½	cup chopped fresh or frozen cranberries
2	tablespoons butter

CAKE LAYERS

1	cup butter, softened
2	cups granulated sugar
4	large eggs
3	cups all-purpose flour
2	teaspoons baking powder
1	teaspoon ground cinnamon
½	teaspoon table salt
½	teaspoon baking soda
½	teaspoon ground ginger
¼	teaspoon ground nutmeg
1½	cups buttermilk
2	teaspoons vanilla extract
	Shortening

APPLE CIDER FROSTING

1	cup apple cider
1	cup butter, softened
¼	teaspoon table salt
1	(32-ounce) package powdered sugar
2	teaspoons vanilla extract
4	to 5 tablespoons whole milk

1 **Prepare the Filling:** Stir together the first 3 ingredients in a small saucepan. Whisk together the cornstarch and cold water in a small bowl until smooth. Stir the cornstarch mixture into cranberry mixture, and cook over medium-low, stirring often, 4 to 5 minutes or until cranberries begin to pop and mixture comes to a boil. Cook, stirring constantly, 1 more minute or until thickened and translucent. Stir in chopped cranberries and butter, and cook, stirring constantly, 1 minute or until butter is melted. Remove from heat and cool completely (about 30 minutes). Cover, and chill 8 to 24 hours.

2 **Prepare Cake Layers:** Preheat the oven to 350°F. In a large mixing bowl beat the 1 cup butter at medium speed with an electric mixer until creamy. Gradually add the 2 cups granulated sugar, beating until light and fluffy. Add eggs, 1 at a time, beating just until blended after each addition.

3 Whisk together the flour and the next 6 ingredients in a medium mixing bowl until well blended. Add flour mixture to butter mixture alternately with buttermilk, beginning and ending with flour mixture. Beat at low speed just until blended after each addition. Stir in the 2 teaspoons vanilla extract. Pour batter into 4 greased (with shortening) and floured 8-inch round cake pans.

4 Bake in the preheated oven 18 to 20 minutes or until a wooden pick inserted in center comes out clean. Cool in pans on wire racks 10 minutes; remove from pans. Cool completely on wire racks (about 1 hour).

5 Meanwhile, prepare Apple Cider Frosting: Cook the cider in a small saucepan over medium, stirring often, 10 to 15 minutes or until reduced to ¼ cup. Cool completely, about 20 minutes.

6 Beat the 1 cup butter and ¼ teaspoon salt in a large mixing bowl with an electric mixer on medium speed until creamy. Gradually add powdered sugar alternately with reduced apple cider, vanilla, and milk, beating well after each addition. If needed, add up to 1 tablespoon milk, 1 teaspoon at a time, and beat until desired consistency is reached.

7 **Assemble Cake:** Place 1 Cake Layer on a cake plate. Spoon 1 cup Apple Cider Frosting into a resealable plastic freezer bag; snip 1 corner to make a small hole. Pipe a ring of frosting around Cake Layer just inside the top edge. Spread Cake Layer with about ⅔ cup chilled Cranberry Filling, spreading to edge of piped frosting. Repeat with 2 more layers. Top with remaining Cake Layer. Spread remaining Frosting over top and sides of cake. Garnish with decorated sugar cones, if desired.

CAKE GARNISH HOW-TO

1. Let 6 to 10 sugar cones stand at room temperature, uncovered, 24 hours. Cut bottoms from several cones to make trees of varying heights.

2. Prepare an extra batch of Apple Cider Frosting. Using 1 cup at a time, place frosting in a resealable plastic freezer bag. Snip one corner to make a ¼-inch hole. Pipe small dots to cover each cone, starting at bottom and lifting up.

3. Carefully press silver dragees into wet frosting. Let cones dry 24 hours. Place around edge and on top of cake.

CLASSIC COCONUT CAKE

The key to the fabulous flavor of this cake is fresh coconut. It takes a little extra time and effort to crack the coconut and remove and shred the meat—but it's worth every minute!

SERVES 16 SERVINGS **HANDS-ON** 1 HOUR, 15 MINUTES **TOTAL** 2 HOURS, 15 MINUTES, INCLUDING 40 MINUTES COOLING

CAKE LAYERS

5	large eggs, at room temperature
1	cup unsalted butter, at room temperature
1	cup whole milk, at room temperature
3	cups sifted cake flour
1	tablespoon baking powder
½	teaspoon kosher salt
	Butter
2	cups granulated sugar
1	tablespoon vanilla

COCONUT

1	fresh coconut, husk and peel removed and grated or finely shredded (3 to 4 cups)

SUGAR SYRUP

2	cups granulated sugar
¼	teaspoon cream of tartar
¾	cup water

FROSTING

3	large egg whites, at room temperature
¼	teaspoon kosher salt
2	teaspoons pure vanilla extract

1 Prepare Cake Layers: Preheat the oven to 350°F. In a medium mixing bowl combine the cake flour, baking powder, and kosher salt. Butter 3 (8×1½-inch) round cake pans; line bottoms with waxed paper. Butter and lightly flour waxed paper.

2 In large mixing bowl beat butter with an electric mixer on medium to high speed 30 seconds. Add the sugar and vanilla; beat on medium speed until well combined, 3 to 4 minutes. Add eggs, 1 at a time, beating well after each addition. Alternately add flour mixture and milk to butter mixture, beating on low after each addition just until combined. Divide batter among the three pans.

3 Bake in the preheated oven until a wooden pick inserted in centers comes out clean, 20 to 25 minutes. Cool in pans on wire racks, 10 minutes. Remove from pans; peel off and discard waxed paper. Cool completely on wire racks, about 30 minutes.

4 Prepare Coconut: With an ice pick or nut pick, make holes in two of the eyes with a pressing, twisting motion. If eyes are especially tough, tap the top of the pick with a hammer. Pour coconut water into a large measuring cup. If desired, cover and save for another use.

5 To crack the coconut shell, hold the coconut in one hand and tap with hammer, rotating coconut as you strike. After 2 to 3 minutes, listen for a change in tapping sound and then a cracking sound, which indicates the shell has split. Separate coconut into pieces, tapping with hammer as necessary.

6 Remove coconut meat to a towel-protected counter. Slowly work thin-bladed knife between coconut and shell. With a vegetable peeler, remove and discard brown skin from coconut. Using the smallest holes on a box grater, shred coconut.

7 Prepare Sugar Syrup: Combine the sugar, cream of tartar, and water in a medium saucepan. Cook over low, stirring often, until sugar is dissolved. Cover the pan, and bring to boiling. Boil 2 minutes. Remove the cover and attach a candy thermometer to pan. Cook, without stirring, until thermometer registers 240°F, 5 to 10 minutes.

8 Prepare the Frosting: Beat the egg whites in a large mixing bowl with an electric mixer on medium to high speed until frothy. Add kosher salt; beat until stiff peaks begin to form. Beat with an electric mixer on low speed, gradually pouring in hot Sugar Syrup. Beat in the vanilla. Beat on medium-high speed until light and fluffy and Frosting holds its shape when a beater is lifted, 3 to 4 minutes.

10 Assemble Cake: Place 1 Cake Layer on a serving plate or stand. Spread Cake Layer with one-third of the Frosting, then sprinkle generously with Coconut. (If Frosting thickens, set over bowl of hot water.) Repeat with the second Cake Layer. Top with remaining Cake Layer, and spread top and sides with remaining Frosting. Gently press remaining coconut onto top and sides of cake.

DULCE DE LECHE CAKE

As impressive as this cake looks—and as delicious as it is—it is not at all difficult to make. The caramel-flavor Dulce de Leche Cream filling is simply made from sweetened condensed milk and prepared dulce de leche that are briefly cooked together.

....

SERVES 12 **HANDS-ON** 1 HOUR **TOTAL** 9 HOURS, 50 MINUTES, INCLUDING 8 HOURS CHILLING

CAKE LAYERS
Shortening

Flour

1   2-layer-size white cake mix
¾   cup butter, softened
5   large eggs
½   cup water
2   tablespoons finely shredded orange peel

DULCE DE LECHE CREAM
1   (14-ounce) can sweetened condensed milk
1   (13.4-ounce) can dulce de leche

WHIPPED CREAM FROSTING
2   tablespoons cold water
1   teaspoon unflavored gelatin
1½ cups whipping cream
3   tablespoons granulated sugar
1   tablespoon orange-flavor liqueur (optional)

CARAMELIZED SUGAR DRIZZLE
(optional)
⅓   cup granulated sugar

1 Prepare the Cake Layers: Preheat the oven to 350°F. Grease (with shortening) and flour 1 (10-inch) springform pan. (If your springform pan does not have a tight fit, line the outside of the pan with foil.) Beat the cake mix, butter, eggs, and water in an extra-large bowl with an electric mixer on low speed until combined. Beat on medium speed 2 minutes more (batter will be thick). Stir in orange peel. Spread batter in prepared pan.

2 Bake in the preheated oven until a wooden pick inserted in center comes out clean, about 40 minutes. Cool in pan on a wire rack 10 minutes (cake may sink slightly during cooling). Loosen cake from side of pan; remove side. Lift cake from pan bottom using a wide metal spatula. Cool cake completely on wire rack, about 30 minutes.

3 Meanwhile, prepare the Dulce de Leche Cream. In a large saucepan combine half of the sweetened condensed milk and the dulce de leche. Bring just to boiling over medium, stirring often. Remove from heat and transfer to a bowl. Cover, and cool 5 minutes.

4 Assemble Cake: Using a long serrated knife, cut the cake in half horizontally to make two Layers. Place 1 Cake Layer, cut side up, on a serving platter. Slide pieces of waxed paper underneath the Cake Layer on all sides to catch drips. Spread ½ to ¾ cup of the Dulce de Leche Cream on top of Layer. Top with the second Cake Layer, cut side up, and press down lightly. Spread ½ to ¾ cup of the Dulce de Leche Cream over the top. Cover, and chill 8 hours. Cover, and chill any remaining Dulce de Leche Cream.

5 Meanwhile, prepare the Whipped Cream Frosting. In a large saucepan bring about 1 inch of water to boiling over high. In a 1-cup heatproof glass measuring cup combine the cold water and gelatin; let stand 2 minutes. Place the measuring cup in the boiling water in saucepan. Cook, stirring, until the gelatin is completely dissolved, about 1 minute. Remove measuring cup from saucepan and cool 5 minutes. Beat whipping cream, sugar, and, if desired, orange-flavor liqueur in a chilled large bowl with the chilled beaters of an electric mixer on medium speed, while gradually drizzling in the gelatin mixture. Beat until stiff peaks form (tips stand straight).

6 Prepare the Caramelized Sugar Drizzle (if using). In a large skillet cook the sugar over medium-high until it starts to melt, shaking skillet occasionally. (Do not stir.) When sugar starts to melt, reduce heat to low, and cook until all of the sugar is melted, stirring as needed with a wooden spoon, about 5 minutes. Remove from heat. Immediately drizzle over frosted cake.

7 Spread Frosting over top and sides of cake. Remove waxed paper pieces from under the cake. Just before serving, (if using) drizzle with Caramelized Sugar Drizzle. Serve with any remaining Dulce de Leche Cream.

WINTER WONDERLAND CAKE

Red edible glitter mixed into the batter and a forest of pink meringue trees on top give this almond-flavor cake holiday flair.

SERVES 16 **HANDS-ON** 1 HOUR **TOTAL** 1 HOUR, 50 MINUTES, INCLUDING 50 MINUTES CHILLING

CAKE LAYERS

- 7 tablespoons unsalted butter, at room temperature
- 1½ cups granulated sugar
- 1¾ cups cake flour
- 2 teaspoons baking powder
- 1 teaspoon table salt
- 5 large egg whites
- ¾ cup milk
- 3 tablespoons canola oil
- 1 teaspoon almond extract
- 2 tablespoons red edible glitter
  Nonstick baking spray

FROSTING

- 5 large egg whites
- 1 cup granulated sugar
  Pinch table salt
- 1 pound unsalted butter, slightly softened
  Powdered sugar

MERINGUE TREES (optional)

- 3 large egg whites
  Pinch table salt
- 1 drop red gel food coloring
- ½ cup superfine sugar

1 Prepare the Cake Layers: Preheat the oven to 325°F. Beat the butter and 1½ cups sugar in a large mixing bowl with an electric mixer on low speed just until combined. Increase speed to high, and beat until light and fluffy.

2 Whisk together the flour, baking powder, and salt in a medium bowl. Whisk together the egg whites, milk, oil, and almond extract in another medium bowl. Add flour mixture, half at a time, alternating with egg mixture and creamed butter. Beat on low speed until smooth after each addition. Fold in edible glitter. Pour batter into a 15×10×1-inch baking pan lined with parchment paper and coated with nonstick spray.

3 Bake in the preheated oven until cake springs back in center when lightly touched, 20 minutes. Cool completely in pan on a wire rack, about 30 minutes.

4 Prepare the Frosting: Continually whisk egg whites, granulated sugar, and salt in a large heatproof mixing bowl set over a pan of simmering water until sugar is dissolved and mixture reaches 160°F. Remove the pan from the heat. Beat with an electric mixer on high speed until stiff peaks form. Add butter, a small piece at a time, until frosting thickens and becomes smooth and spreadable. (If it begins to curdle, continue to whisk, and add another small piece of butter until smooth.)

5 Prepare the Meringue Trees (if using): Preheat the oven to 250°F. Beat egg whites, salt, and food coloring in a large mixing bowl with an electric mixer on high speed until foamy. Add the sugar, 1 tablespoon at a time. Beat until stiff peaks form. Transfer to a pastry bag fitted with a ¼-inch star tip. Pipe a star onto a parchment-lined baking sheet. Rotating tip slightly, pipe a smaller star on the first star. Continue adding layers until tree is 3 to 4 inches high, lifting tip to finish with a peak. Repeat to make 2- to 3-inch-high trees, spacing 1 inch apart on the baking sheet. Bake taller trees just until baked through, about 65 minutes, and shorter trees about 55 minutes. Turn off oven. Let meringues dry in oven with door closed, 1 hour.

6 Assemble Cake: Cut the cake in half lengthwise and crosswise to create four 5×7½-inch rectangles. Place one Layer of cake on a stand or plate. Spread with an even layer of Frosting, about ¾ cup. Repeat until all Cake Layers are stacked. (There will be extra frosting.) Freeze 20 minutes to set. Spread remaining Frosting over the cake. Chill 30 minutes. Decorate with Meringue Trees, if using. Sprinkle with powdered sugar.

RED VELVET CHEESECAKE-VANILLA CAKE WITH CREAM CHEESE FROSTING

Red velvet cake is a staple on holiday tables across the South, and this is our favorite take on it: two layers of creamy red velvet cheesecake with moist vanilla cake in the middle, all blanketed in a cream cheese frosting. Don't skip the crumb coat of frosting, which keeps the red velvet layer from showing through the frosting.

SERVES 16 **HANDS-ON** 1 HOUR **TOTAL** 12 HOURS, INCLUDING 9 HOURS, 10 MINUTES COOLING AND CHILLING

CHEESECAKE LAYERS

Shortening
4½ (8-ounce) packages cream cheese, softened
2¼ cups granulated sugar
6 large eggs, lightly beaten
1½ cups sour cream
¾ cup whole buttermilk
4½ tablespoons unsweetened cocoa
2 (1-ounce) bottles liquid red food coloring
1 tablespoon vanilla extract
1½ teaspoons distilled white vinegar

VANILLA CAKE LAYER

½ cup salted butter, softened
1 cup granulated sugar
1½ cups bleached cake flour
2 teaspoons baking powder
¼ teaspoon table salt
⅔ cup whole milk
1½ teaspoons vanilla extract
3 large egg whites
Shortening

CREAM CHEESE FROSTING

2 (8-ounce) packages cream cheese, softened
½ cup salted butter, softened
1 (32-ounce) package powdered sugar
2 teaspoons vanilla extract

1 Prepare the Cheesecake Layers: Preheat the oven to 325°F. Line bottom and sides of 2 (9-inch) round pans with aluminum foil, allowing 2 to 3 inches to extend over sides; lightly grease foil (with shortening). Beat the cream cheese and granulated sugar in a large bowl with an electric mixer on medium speed just until combined, about 1 minute. Add the eggs, sour cream, buttermilk, cocoa, red food coloring, vanilla, and vinegar, beating on low speed just until combined, about 4 minutes. (Do not overbeat.) Pour batter into prepared pans.

2 Bake in preheated oven 10 minutes; reduce heat to 300°F, and bake until center is slightly jiggly, about 1 hour and 5 minutes. Turn oven off. Let Cheesecake Layers stand in oven 30 minutes. Remove pans from oven; cool in pans on wire racks 1 hour. Cover, and chill 8 hours.

3 Prepare the Vanilla Cake Layer: Preheat oven to 325°F. Beat the butter in a medium bowl with an electric mixer on medium speed until creamy; gradually add granulated sugar, beating until light and fluffy, about 5 minutes.

4 Stir together the flour, baking powder, and salt in a bowl; add to the butter mixture alternately with the milk, beginning and ending with the flour mixture. Beat on low speed just until blended after each addition. Stir in the vanilla.

5 Beat the egg whites in a clean bowl with an electric mixer fitted with whisk attachment on high speed until stiff peaks form; fold about one-third of egg whites into batter. Gradually fold in the remaining egg whites. Pour batter into 1 (9-inch) greased (with shortening) and floured round cake pan.

6 Bake in the preheated oven until a wooden pick inserted in center comes out clean, 33 to 36 minutes. Cool in pan on a wire rack 10 minutes. Remove from pan to wire rack; cool completely, about 30 minutes.

7 Prepare the Cream Cheese Frosting: Beat the cream cheese and butter with an electric mixer on medium speed until creamy, about 5 minutes. Gradually add the powdered sugar, beating at low speed until blended after each addition; stir in vanilla. Increase speed to medium, and beat until light and fluffy.

8 Assemble Cake: Lift Cheesecake Layers from pans, using foil sides as handles. Place 1 Cheesecake Layer, bottom side up, on a cake plate. Place Vanilla Cake Layer on Cheesecake Layer. (This layer will be slightly taller than the Cheesecake Layers; trim the top of the layer, if desired.) Top Vanilla Cake Layer with the remaining Cheesecake Layer, bottom side up. Spread a thin layer of Cream Cheese Frosting over top and sides of cake to seal in crumbs. Chill cake 20 minutes. Spread remaining frosting over top and sides of cake.

RED VELVET CAKE

*If you're up for a more traditional take on Red Velvet Cake than the one offered on the previous page,
look no further than this classic recipe.*

SERVES 16 **HANDS-ON** 1 HOUR **TOTAL** 2 HOURS, INCLUDING 40 MINUTES COOLING

CAKE LAYERS

3 large eggs, at room temperature
¾ cup butter, at room temperature
  Shortening, at room temperature
2½ cups granulated sugar
1 (1-ounce) bottle red food coloring
1½ teaspoons vanilla extract
3 cups all-purpose flour
1 tablespoon unsweetened
  cocoa powder
¾ teaspoon table salt
1½ cups buttermilk or sour milk
1½ teaspoons baking soda
1½ teaspoons vinegar

CREAMY WHITE FROSTING

½ cup shortening
½ cup butter
1½ teaspoons vanilla extract
½ teaspoon almond extract
4 cups powdered sugar
3 to 4 tablespoons milk

GARNISH

Round peppermint candy,
some broken

1 Prepare the Cheesecake Layers: Preheat the oven to 350°F. Lightly grease (with shortening) and flour 3 (8-inch) round cake pans.

2 Beat the butter in an extra-large bowl with an electric mixer on medium to high speed for 30 seconds. Gradually add the sugar, about ¼ cup at a time, beating on medium speed until combined. Beat 2 minutes more. Add eggs, one at a time, beating well after each addition. Beat in food coloring and vanilla. Stir together the flour, cocoa powder, and salt in a medium bowl. Add flour mixture alternately with buttermilk, beating on low speed after each addition just until combined. In a small bowl stir together baking soda and vinegar; fold into batter. Spread batter into prepared pans.

3 Bake in the preheated oven until a wooden pick inserted near centers comes out clean, 22 to 25 minutes. Cool Cake Layers in pans on wire racks 10 minutes. Remove Cake Layers from pans; cool completely on wire racks, about 30 minutes.

4 Prepare Creamy White Frosting: Beat the shortening, butter, vanilla, and almond extract in a large bowl with an electric mixer on medium speed 30 seconds. Gradually add 2 cups of the powdered sugar, beating until well combined. Beat in 2 tablespoons milk. Gradually beat in the remaining 2 cups powdered sugar. Beat in 1 to 2 tablespoons milk until Frosting reaches a spreading consistency.

5 Assemble Cake: Place 1 Cake Layer, bottom side up, on a cake plate. Spread Cake Layer with ¾ cup Frosting; repeat with 1 more layer. Top with remaining Cake Layer. Spread top and sides with remaining Frosting. Decorate top and bottom edge of cake with peppermint candy.

CRANBERRY-VANILLA BEAN CAKE WITH LEMON CREAM CHEESE FROSTING

A sweet-tart Cranberry Filling and Lemon Cream Cheese Frosting are the special additions that make this cake taste like it came from a fancy bakery.

SERVES 14 **HANDS-ON** 35 MINUTES **TOTAL** 1 HOUR, 55 MINUTES

CAKE LAYERS
- 6 egg whites, lightly beaten
- 1 cup buttermilk
- 1 vanilla bean, split lengthwise
- 2¼ cups cake flour
- 1¾ cups granulated sugar
- 4 teaspoons baking powder
- 1 teaspoon table salt
- ¾ cup butter, softened
  Shortening

CRANBERRY FILLING
- 1 (12-ounce) package fresh or frozen cranberries, thawed
- ½ cup sugar
- 2 teaspoons orange zest
- 2 tablespoons orange juice
- ¼ teaspoon ground cinnamon
- ⅛ teaspoon ground ginger
- ⅛ teaspoon ground cloves

LEMON CREAM CHEESE FROSTING
- 2 (8-ounce) packages cream cheese, softened
- ¾ cup butter, softened
- 3½ cups powdered sugar
- 1 tablespoon lemon zest
- 1 tablespoon lemon juice
- 1 tablespoon milk

WHITE CHOCOLATE CURLS (optional)
- 1½ ounces white chocolate (not baking pieces)
- 1 teaspoon shortening

1 Prepare the Cake Layers: Preheat the oven to 350°F. Combine the egg whites and buttermilk in a small bowl. Using the tip of a small sharp knife, scrape seeds from vanilla bean. Stir seeds into buttermilk mixture. Let stand at room temperature 30 minutes. Meanwhile, in a bowl stir together the cake flour, sugar, baking powder, and salt.

2 Beat the butter in a large mixing bowl with an electric mixer on medium to high speed 30 seconds. Gradually stir in the flour mixture until mixture resembles coarse crumbs. Stir in half of the buttermilk mixture until moistened. Add the remaining buttermilk mixture. Beat with an electric mixer on medium speed 2 minutes. Pour batter into 2 (9×1½-inch) round cake pans greased (with shortening) and lightly floured, spreading evenly.

3 Bake in the preheated oven until a wooden pick inserted near centers comes out clean, 25 to 30 minutes. Cool in pans on wire racks 10 minutes. Remove layers from pans; cool completely on wire racks.

4 Prepare the Cranberry Filling: In a medium saucepan combine the cranberries, sugar, orange zest and juice, cinnamon, ginger, and cloves. Bring to boiling; reduce heat. Simmer, uncovered, until cranberries pop and filling starts to thicken, about 10 minutes. Lightly mash cranberries with the back of a spoon or a potato masher. Transfer filling to a bowl; cool completely.

5 Prepare the Lemon Cream Cheese Frosting: Beat the cream cheese and butter in a large mixing bowl with an electric mixer on medium speed until light and fluffy, 3 to 5 minutes. Gradually beat in 1 cup of the powdered sugar. Beat in the lemon zest and juice. Gradually beat in remaining 2½ cups powdered sugar. If necessary, beat in milk, 1 tablespoon at a time, to reach spreading consistency.

6 Prepare the White Chocolate Curls (if using): Place the white chocolate and shortening in a small, heavy saucepan. Melt over low heat, stirring constantly. Use an offset metal spatula to evenly spread the chocolate in a glass baking dish. Let stand until set. To make the curls, hold a straightedge metal spatula against the baking dish just inside the edge of the chocolate at a 45-degree angle. Apply gentle, steady pressure, and push the spatula straight forward. For looser curls, push a spatula forward in an arc. Lift any curls with a wooden skewer to avoid fingerprints in the chocolate. Use immediately or place a single layer on paper towels in a storage container. Cover and store at room temperature or chill.

7 Assemble Cake: Cut each Cake Layer in half horizontally. Place 1 Cake Layer, cut side up, on a serving plate; spread with one-third of the cranberry filling. Top with a second Cake Layer; spread with ¾ cup of the Lemon Cream Cheese Frosting. Spread one-third of the Cranberry Filling on frosting. Top with a third Cake Layer; spread with the remaining Cranberry Filling. Top with the fourth Cake Layer, cut side down. Frost top and sides of cake with the remaining Frosting. If desired, garnish with White Chocolate Curls

DUTCH MOCHA CHOCOLATE CAKE

The fabulous frosting for this rich cake is called Unforgettable White Chocolate Frosting for a very good reason. It is made with melted white chocolate, cream cheese, and butter.

SERVES 16 **HANDS-ON** 40 MINUTES **TOTAL** 1 HOUR, 25 MINUTES, INCLUDING 30 MINUTES COOLING

CAKE LAYERS

- ¾ cup unsweetened cocoa powder
- 2¾ cups granulated sugar
- 1 cup very strong hot coffee
- 3 cups sifted cake flour
- 1 teaspoon baking soda
- ½ teaspoon table salt
- 1 cup butter
- 2 teaspoons vanilla extract
- 1 (8-ounce) carton sour cream
- 5 egg whites
  Shortening

WHITE CHOCOLATE FROSTING

- 18 ounces chopped white chocolate baking squares or bars
- 1 (3-ounce) package cream cheese, softened
- 1½ cups butter, cut into pieces

1 Prepare the Cake Layers: Preheat the oven to 350°F. Stir together the cocoa powder and ¾ cup of the sugar in a medium bowl. Gradually whisk in coffee until sugar is dissolved. Cool to room temperature.

2 In a large mixing bowl beat the butter with an electric mixer on medium speed 30 seconds. Add 1 cup of the sugar and vanilla; beat until well combined. Whisk or stir the sour cream into the cooled cocoa-coffee mixture. Sift together the cake flour, baking soda, and salt. Alternately add flour mixture with cocoa mixture to the creamed butter mixture, beating after each addition until just combined.

3 Using clean beaters, in a large mixing bowl beat the egg whites on medium-high until soft peaks form, about 1 minute. Gradually add the remaining 1 cup sugar, and beat on high until stiff peaks form. Gently fold about one-third of the egg white mixture into creamed mixture to lighten. Fold in remaining egg white mixture.

4 Pour batter into 3 (9×1½-inch) round baking pans greased (with shortening) and lightly floured. Bake in the preheated oven until a wooden pick inserted near centers comes out clean, 25 to 30 minutes. Cool Cake Layers in pans on wire racks 10 minutes. Remove the Cake Layers from pans and cool completely on wire racks, about 30 minutes.

5 Prepare the White Chocolate Frosting: In a heavy saucepan melt the white chocolate over low. Cool until slightly warm. Beat the cream cheese in a large mixing bowl with an electric mixer on medium-high speed until smooth. Add the butter to the cream cheese; beat until fluffy, 3 to 4 minutes. Gradually add the cooled white chocolate; beat until well blended.

6 Assemble Cake: Place 1 Cake Layer on a cake plate; spread with about ½ cup Frosting. Repeat with a second Cake Layer. Top with the third Cake Layer; frost top and sides with the remaining Frosting. If desired, pipe Frosting around top and bottom edges of the cake. Serve immediately, or cover loosely and store in the refrigerator. Let chilled cake stand at room temperature 30 minutes before serving.

CRANBERRY LAYER CAKE

To make the sugared cranberries that top this simple but beautiful cake, bring ¼ cup each sugar and water to a simmer in a small saucepan just until the sugar is dissolved. Remove from the heat, and add ½ cup fresh cranberries, shaking to coat. Let stand 10 minutes. Strain the cranberries, and let dry on a parchment-lined wire rack 1 hour. Place cranberries and ¼ cup granulated sugar in a resealable plastic bag, and shake gently until all of the cranberries are coated.

SERVES 12 **HANDS-ON** 25 MINUTES **TOTAL** 1 HOUR, 20 MINUTES INCLUDING 30 MINUTES COOLING

CAKE LAYERS

- 2 cups fresh or frozen cranberries
- 1 (2-layer-size) package white cake mix
- 1 cup water
- ⅓ cup vegetable oil
- 3 large eggs
- 1¼ cups chopped pecans, toasted
- 1 tablespoon orange zest
- Shortening

FROSTING

- 1 (8-ounce) package cream cheese, softened
- ½ cup butter, softened
- 1 teaspoon vanilla
- 4¾ to 5½ cups powdered sugar
- ½ teaspoon orange zest

1 Prepare the Cake Layers: Preheat the oven to 350°F. Rinse the cranberries in cold water; drain, then coarsely chop.

2 Combine the cake mix, water, oil, and eggs in a large bowl. Beat with an electric mixer on low speed just until combined. Increase speed to medium and beat 2 minutes. Fold in cranberries, 1 cup of the pecans, and orange zest. Pour batter into 2 (8×1½-inch or 9×1½-inch) round cake pans greased (with shortening) and floured.

3 Bake in the preheated oven until a wooden pick inserted near centers comes out clean, 25 to 30 minutes for 9-inch layer or 30 to 35 minutes for 8-inch layer. Cool in pans on wire racks 10 minutes. Remove layers from pans; cool completely on wire racks, about 30 minutes.

4 Prepare the Frosting: Beat the cream cheese, butter, and vanilla in a large bowl with an electric mixer on medium speed until light and fluffy, 4 to 5 minutes. Gradually beat in enough powdered sugar to reach spreading consistency. Stir in orange zest.

5 Assemble Cake: Place 1 Cake Layer on a cake plate. Spread with about ½ cup of the frosting. Top with second Cake Layer. Spread top and sides of cake with remaining frosting. Sprinkle top with the remaining ¼ cup pecans. Serve immediately, or cover loosely and store in the refrigerator. Let chilled cake stand at room temperature 30 minutes before serving.

POLKA-DOT CAKE

It looks like magic, but it's not! The polka-dot effect in this whimsical cake is easily achieved by making Red Velvet-flavor cake balls from a mix and then staggering them in the batter of a from-scratch white cake before baking. This delightful look will inspire oohs and ahhs!

SERVES 16 **HANDS-ON** 1 HOUR **TOTAL** 4 HOURS, 10 MINUTES

CAKE BALLS
Shortening
1   (2-layer-size) package white cake mix
2   tablespoons cocoa powder
1   (1-ounce) bottle liquid red food coloring

CAKE
6   egg whites
3   cups all-purpose flour
1½ teaspoons baking powder
1   teaspoon table salt
½   teaspoon baking soda
¾   cup shortening
2⅔ cups granulated sugar
1½ teaspoons vanilla
2   cups buttermilk

VANILLA BUTTERCREAM FROSTING
1½ cups unsalted butter, softened
1   (16-ounce) jar marshmallow creme
½   cup powdered sugar
1   teaspoon vanilla extract

SUGARED CRANBERRIES (optional)
¼   cup granulated sugar
¼   cup water
½   cup fresh cranberries
Fresh mint leaves

1   Prepare the Cake Balls: Preheat the oven to 350°F. Grease (with shortening) and flour the top and bottom cups of 1 (12-cup) cake-pop pan. Prepare the cake mix batter, adding the cocoa powder according to package directions. Beat in food coloring. Spoon 1 tablespoon of the batter into each bottom cup (without hole), filling each full. Place top half of pan on top, and secure.

2   Bake in the preheated oven until a wooden pick inserted into holes comes out clean, about 10 minutes. Cool in pan on a wire rack 5 minutes. Remove top pan. Remove cake balls from pans; cool completely on wire rack. Wash, grease, and flour pan; repeat baking twice to make 36 cake balls total. (Cover, and chill remaining batter to use for cupcakes, following package directions. Makes 12 cupcakes.)

3   Meanwhile, prepare the Cake: Place the egg whites in a small bowl; cover and let stand at room temperature 30 minutes. Grease (with shortening) and flour 1 (10-inch) tube pan with a removable bottom. Stir together the flour, baking powder, salt, and baking soda in a medium bowl. Beat shortening in an extra-large mixing bowl with an electric mixer on medium to high speed 30 seconds. Add the sugar and vanilla. Beat until light, about 3 minutes. Add the egg whites, one at a time, beating well after each addition. Alternately add flour mixture and buttermilk to beaten mixture, beating on low speed after each addition just until combined.

4   Arrange half of the cake balls, staggered, in the prepared tube pan to give the baked cake a polka-dot effect. Spoon about 4 cups of the cake batter over the balls. Arrange remaining cake balls, staggered, in the pan. Spoon the remaining batter over cake balls. Place tube pan on a baking sheet. Bake until a long wooden skewer inserted into cake comes out clean, 60 to 70 minutes. Remove, and cool on a wire rack 10 minutes. Run a sharp knife around the sides and tube, and along the bottom to loosen the cake from the pan. Invert cake onto a cake plate; remove pan. Cool on a wire rack until completely cooled, about 2 hours.

5   Prepare the Vanilla Buttercream Frosting: Beat the butter in a large mixing bowl with an electric mixer on medium speed until light and fluffy, 3 to 4 minutes. Add the marshmallow creme; beat until smooth. Add the powdered sugar and vanilla; beat until light and fluffy. (If frosting is too stiff to spread, soften in microwave no longer than 10 seconds, then beat again until light and fluffy.)

6   Prepare the Sugared Cranberries (if using): Bring the sugar and water to a simmer in a small saucepan just until the sugar is dissolved. Remove from the heat and add the fresh cranberries, shaking to coat. Let stand 10 minutes. Strain the cranberries, and let dry on a parchment-lined wire rack 1 hour. Place cranberries and ¼ cup sugar in a resealable plastic bag, and shake gently until cranberries are coated.

7   Assemble Cake: Place cake on a serving platter. Spread Frosting on cake (and cupcakes). If desired, garnish with sugared cranberries and fresh mint leaves.

COCONUT LAYER CAKE

The slightly tart Crème Fraîche Frosting offers a nice counterpoint to this sweet Southern-style cake.

SERVES 16 **HANDS-ON** 45 MINUTES **TOTAL** 4 HOURS, 45 MINUTES, INCLUDING 2 HOUR, 10 MINUTES COOLING

CAKE LAYERS

2 cups all-purpose flour
1½ teaspoons baking powder
¼ teaspoon table salt
4 large eggs, at room temperature
2 cups granulated sugar
1 cup milk
¼ cup butter
1½ teaspoons vanilla
  Shortening

COCONUT FILLING

1¼ cups whipping cream
¾ cup granulated sugar
½ cup butter, cut up
1 tablespoon cornstarch
1 tablespoon water
  Pinch table salt
2 cups flaked or shredded coconut
½ teaspoon vanilla extract

CRÈME FRAÎCHE FROSTING

1 (7-ounce) jar crème fraîche or
  1 (8-ounce) container sour cream
1 cup whipping cream
¾ cup powdered sugar
½ teaspoon vanilla extract

GARNISH (optional)

Fresh coconut curls, toasted

1 Prepare the Cake Layers: Preheat the oven to 350°F. Stir the together flour, baking powder, and salt in a medium bowl. Beat the eggs in a large mixing bowl with an electric mixer on high speed 4 minutes or until thick. Gradually beat in the sugar on medium speed until light and fluffy, 4 to 5 minutes. Add the flour mixture; beat on low just until combined (mixture will be thick).

2 Heat the milk and butter in a small saucepan over low, stirring, until butter melts; stir in vanilla. Add to batter; beat with an electric mixer on medium speed until combined (batter will be thin). Pour batter into 2 (9×1½-inch or 8×1½-inch) round cake pans greased (with shortening) and lightly floured.

4 Bake in the preheated oven until a wooden pick inserted in centers comes out clean, 25 to 30 minutes. Cool in pans on wire racks 10 minutes. Remove layers from pans; cool completely on wire racks.

5 Prepare the Coconut Filling: Combine the whipping cream, sugar, and butter in a medium saucepan. Bring to boiling, stirring until sugar dissolves. Stir together the cornstarch, water, and salt in a small bowl. Stir into cream mixture; bring to boiling. Cook, stirring, until thick, about 1 minute. Remove from heat. Stir in the coconut and vanilla. Transfer to a medium bowl. Cover the surface with plastic wrap. Chill 2 hours.

6 Prepare the Crème Fraîche Frosting: Combine the crème fraîche, whipping cream, powdered sugar, and vanilla in a large mixing bowl. Beat with an electric mixer on medium speed until mixture is thick and soft peaks form.

7 Assemble Cake: Cut the Cake Layers in half horizontally to make four layers. Place the first layer on a serving plate, cut side up. Spread about ¾ cup of the Coconut Filling over the first Cake Layer. Repeat with two more layers and the remaining Coconut Filling. Top with the remaining Cake Layer. Frost top and sides of cake with Crème Fraîche Frosting. If desired, top cake with coconut curls. Store cake, covered, in the refrigerator up to 24 hours.

White Chocolate–Almond
Reindeer Antlers
recipe on page 101

Peppermint–Dipped
Mocha Butter Cookies
recipe on page 104

Chocolate–Orange Peepholes
recipe on page 102

Pistachio–Orange Snickerdoodles
recipe on page 103

Salted Dulce de Leche
Sandwich Cookies
recipe on page 100

HOLIDAY COOKIES

Christmas just isn't complete without a cookie-baking session or two.
It's a joyful tradition with a sweet payoff, plus there are
always extras for giving.

SALTED DULCE DE LECHE SANDWICH COOKIES

Dulce de leche is caramel made from cream and sugar simmered for seven hours. Since you're kind of busy this time of year, this recipe uses the ready-made variety. Photo page 98.

MAKES 20 SANDWICH COOKIES **HANDS-ON** 45 MINUTES **TOTAL** 3 HOURS, 20 MINUTES

1   cup all-purpose flour
1   cup cornstarch
¼   teaspoon baking powder
¼   teaspoon baking soda
½   cup, plus 2 tablespoons salted butter, softened
½   cup granulated sugar
2   large egg yolks
1   tablespoon bourbon
1   teaspoon lemon zest (from 1 lemon)
1   teaspoon vanilla extract
7   tablespoons canned dulce de leche
2   teaspoons flaky sea salt (such as Maldon)
    Powdered sugar

1 Stir together the flour, cornstarch, baking powder, and baking soda in a medium bowl; set aside.

2 Beat the butter and sugar with a heavy-duty electric stand mixer on medium until creamy. Reduce the speed to medium-low, and add the egg yolks, 1 at a time, beating until combined after each addition. Add the bourbon, zest, and vanilla, beating until well blended. Gradually add the flour mixture to the butter mixture, beating on low just until the dough comes together.

3 Halve the dough; pat each half into a 4-inch disk. Wrap each disk in plastic wrap; chill 2 hours or up to 5 days.

4 Preheat the oven to 350°F. Unwrap 1 dough disk, and place on a lightly floured surface. Roll the dough to ¼-inch thickness. Using a floured 2½-inch scalloped round cutter, cut the cookies from dough, rerolling the scraps once. Place the cookies on the parchment paper-lined baking sheets. Bake in the preheated oven until golden brown around edges, 10 to 11 minutes. Cool on baking sheets on wire racks 2 minutes; transfer the cookies to racks to cool completely, about 20 minutes. Repeat the procedure with the second dough disk.

5 Spread 1 teaspoon dulce de leche on half of the cookies. Sprinkle salt evenly over the top. Top with the remaining cookies, flat sides down. Using a fine wire-mesh strainer, dust the cookies with powdered sugar.

WHITE CHOCOLATE-ALMOND REINDEER ANTLERS

These couldn't be cuter. White chocolate "spackle" keeps sprinkles and nuts in place in the tastiest way.
Photo page 98.

MAKES 4 DOZEN **HANDS-ON** 1 HOUR, 30 MINUTES **TOTAL** 4 HOURS

1½ cups salted butter, softened
1½ cups granulated sugar
2   large eggs
½   teaspoon almond extract
½   teaspoon vanilla extract
3½ cups all-purpose flour
6   ounces white chocolate chips
      (about 1 cup)
      Sliced toasted almonds, edible
      metallic gold glitter sprinkles, small
      red nonpareils

1 Beat the butter with a heavy-duty electric stand mixer on medium until creamy, about 1 minute. Gradually add the granulated sugar, beating until light and fluffy, about 1 minute. Reduce to medium-low; add eggs, 1 at a time, beating until blended after each addition. Add the almond and vanilla extracts; beat just until combined. Gradually add the flour to the butter mixture, beating until blended, about 1 minute. Divide the dough in half, and pat each into an 8-inch-wide disk. Wrap each disk in plastic wrap; chill until firm, 2 hours or up to 5 days.

2 Preheat the oven to 325°F. Unwrap 1 dough disk, and place on a lightly floured surface; roll to ¼-inch thickness. Using a reindeer-shape cutter, cut shapes from the dough. Place 2 inches apart on parchment paper-lined baking sheets. Chill until firm, 10 to 30 minutes.

3 Bake the chilled cookies in batches in the preheated oven until the edges are lightly golden and centers are pale, 10 to 12 minutes, rotating the baking sheets on the racks halfway through the baking time.

4 Cool the cookies on the baking sheets 2 minutes; transfer to wire racks to cool completely, about 20 minutes.

5 Microwave the white chocolate chips in a microwavable bowl on MEDIUM (50% power) until melted, 1½ minutes, stirring every 30 seconds. Dip antler, hoof, and tail portions in melted chocolate; place on wire racks. Arrange almonds on melted chocolate on antler portion of cookies. Sprinkle gold glitter on melted chocolate on hoof and tail portions of cookies. Place a dot of melted chocolate on the nose portion of cookies, and top with a nonpareil. Chill until chocolate sets, about 10 minutes.

CHOCOLATE-ORANGE PEEPHOLES

Swedish pearl sugar is a type of finishing sugar for baked confections that will not melt in the heat of the oven, so it retains its round shape. Photo page 98.

....

MAKES 42 COOKIES **HANDS-ON** 40 MINUTES **TOTAL** 3 HOURS, 30 MINUTES, INCLUDING 2 HOURS CHILLING

1   **cup unsalted butter**

1   **cup powdered sugar**

1   **teaspoon vanilla extract**

2   **cups all-purpose flour, plus more for dusting work surface**

⅓   **cup unsweetened cocoa**

½   **teaspoon kosher salt**

½   **cup Swedish pearl sugar**

¾   **cup, plus 2 tablespoons orange marmalade**

1   Beat the butter and powdered sugar with a heavy-duty electric stand mixer on medium speed until creamy, about 2 minutes. Add the vanilla, and beat just until blended. Stir together the flour, cocoa, and salt in a medium bowl. Gradually add the flour mixture to the butter mixture, beating on low speed just until combined.

2   Divide the dough in half, and pat each into a 5-inch disk. Wrap each disk in plastic wrap; chill 2 hours.

3   Unwrap 1 dough disk, and place on a lightly floured work surface. Roll the disk to ¼-inch thickness. Using a 2-inch round cutter, cut the cookies from the dough, rerolling scraps as necessary. Using a ¾-inch round cutter, cut holes in centers of half of the cookies, leaving remaining half cookies whole. Place the whole cookies on parchment paper-lined baking sheets. Sprinkle cookies with holes in centers evenly with ¼ cup of the pearl sugar; place on parchment-lined baking sheets. Bake in the preheated oven until bottoms are slightly firm, 10 to 11 minutes. Cool on baking sheets 2 minutes; transfer to wire racks to cool completely, about 20 minutes. Repeat the procedure with the second dough disk and remaining ¼ cup pearl sugar.

4   Spoon 1 teaspoon orange marmalade onto the centers of each whole cookie. Top with sugared cookies, flat sides down, to make sandwiches.

PISTACHIO-ORANGE SNICKERDOODLES

Pistachios and cardamom give this riff on the snickerdoodle a touch of far-flung flavor (say those last three words ten times fast). Photo page 98.

MAKES 3 DOZEN **HANDS-ON** 30 MINUTES **TOTAL** 1 HOUR, 15 MINUTES

2¼ cups all-purpose flour

½ teaspoon baking soda

½ teaspoon cream of tartar

½ teaspoon kosher salt

½ teaspoon orange zest (from 1 orange)

½ cup unsalted butter, softened

½ cup canola oil

½ cup powdered sugar

½ cup, plus 2 tablespoons granulated sugar

1 large egg

1 teaspoon vanilla extract

¼ cup shelled raw pistachios

¼ teaspoon ground cardamom

1 Preheat the oven to 350°F. Whisk together the flour, baking soda, cream of tartar, salt, and orange zest in a medium bowl. Set aside.

2 Beat the butter, oil, powdered sugar, and ½ cup of the granulated sugar in a heavy-duty electric stand mixer fitted with the paddle attachment on medium speed until smooth and glossy, 2 to 3 minutes. Add the egg and vanilla; beat until combined, about 30 seconds. Add the flour mixture; beat on low speed until fully combined, 1 to 2 minutes. Cover, and chill 20 to 30 minutes.

3 Combine the pistachios, cardamom, and remaining 2 tablespoons granulated sugar in a mini food processor; pulse until the pistachios are ground, about 15 times. Transfer the mixture to a shallow dish. Using a 1½-tablespoon scoop, scoop the chilled dough into balls, and roll each ball in the pistachio mixture. Place about 2 inches apart on the parchment paper-lined baking sheets. Bake in the preheated oven until barely golden and still mostly pale, about 10 minutes. Cool on the baking sheets on wire racks 5 minutes; transfer the cookies to wire racks to cool completely.

PEPPERMINT-DIPPED MOCHA BUTTER COOKIES

A decadent dipped cookie that's perfect for biscotti-style dunking. Photo page 98.

MAKES 20 COOKIES **HANDS-ON** 30 MINUTES **TOTAL** 3 HOURS, 30 MINUTES, INCLUDING 2 HOURS CHILLING

2   teaspoons hot water
1   teaspoon instant
    espresso granules
1   cup salted butter
½   cup powdered sugar
1   teaspoon peppermint extract
2   cups all-purpose flour
⅓   cup unsweetened cocoa
8   ounces bittersweet chocolate
    baking bar, finely chopped
2   teaspoons coconut oil
2   teaspoons light corn syrup
⅓   cup crushed candy canes (about
    2¼ ounces)

1   Stir together the hot water and espresso powder in a small bowl until
    espresso dissolves.

2   Beat the butter and powdered sugar in a medium bowl with a heavy-duty
    electric stand mixer on medium-low speed until smooth, about 2 minutes. Beat in
    the espresso mixture and peppermint extract until combined. Whisk together the
    flour and cocoa in a medium bowl. Add the flour mixture to the butter mixture;
    beat on low speed until well combined.

3   Turn the dough out onto a sheet of plastic wrap. Shape the dough into a 5-inch-
    long, 2½-inch-wide, 1-inch-high rectangle. Wrap the dough rectangle tightly with
    plastic wrap, and chill 2 hours.

4   Preheat the oven to 350°F. Unwrap the dough rectangle. Using a sharp knife, cut
    the dough crosswise into 20 (¼-inch-thick) slices, and place on parchment paper-
    lined baking sheets 1 inch apart. Bake in the preheated oven until cookies are
    set, about 10 minutes. Cool on baking sheets on wire racks 3 minutes; transfer the
    cookies to wire racks to cool completely, about 20 minutes.

5   Microwave the bittersweet chocolate and coconut oil in a small microwavable
    bowl on HIGH until melted and smooth, 1 minute, stirring every 30 seconds. Stir in
    the corn syrup. Dip 1 end of cooled cookies, 1 at a time, in the melted chocolate,
    and place on parchment-lined baking sheets. Sprinkle melted chocolate with
    crushed candy canes. Chill until set, about 5 minutes, or let stand at room
    temperature until set, about 20 minutes.

SPICED RUM BALLS

Simple and spirited, these are a nice change of pace from the usual truffles or bourbon balls.
Photo page 106.

....

MAKES ABOUT 4 DOZEN **HANDS-ON** 20 MINUTES **TOTAL** 9 HOURS, 20 MINUTES, INCLUDING 8 HOURS CHILLING

2   (8.8-ounce) packages Biscoff
    cookies, finely crushed
1   cup powdered sugar, plus more for
    coating rum balls
2½ tablespoons unsweetened cocoa
1⅓ cups chopped pecans, toasted
⅔   cup spiced rum
3   tablespoons light corn syrup

1   Combine the cookies, powdered sugar, and cocoa in a food processor; pulse until finely ground, about 20 seconds. Transfer to a large bowl, and stir in the pecans.

2   Stir together the rum and corn syrup in a separate bowl until well blended. Add the rum mixture to the cookie mixture; stir to combine. Cover and chill until firm, about 1 hour. Shape the mixture into 1-inch balls, and roll balls in powdered sugar. Cover and chill 8 hours or overnight. Store the rum balls in an airtight container in the refrigerator up to 2 weeks.

Raspberry-Lime Swirl Bars
recipe on page 107

Benne Seed Tuile *recipe on page 107*

Spiced Rum Balls *recipe on page 105*

RASPBERRY-LIME SWIRL BARS

These marbleized, mouthwatering confections are perfect for the holidays.

MAKES 2 DOZEN **HANDS-ON** 40 MINUTES **TOTAL** 4 HOURS, 40 MINUTES, INCLUDING 4 HOURS CHILLING

1   (10-ounce) package shortbread cookies, finely crushed (about 2 cups)

6   tablespoons salted butter, melted

1   tablespoon powdered sugar

1   cup granulated sugar

¾   cup fresh lime juice (from 5 to 6 limes)

¼   cup cornstarch

3   large egg yolks

2   large eggs

½   cup cold salted butter, diced

¼   cup seedless raspberry jam

1   Line a 9-inch square metal baking pan with aluminum foil, allowing 2 to 3 inches to hang over sides. Spray the sides and bottom of the prepared pan with cooking spray. Process the crushed shortbread cookies, melted butter, and powdered sugar in a food processor until finely ground, about 20 seconds. Press the mixture evenly into the bottom of the pan; cover and chill 2 hours.

2   Preheat the oven to 350°F. Combine the granulated sugar, lime juice, cornstarch, egg yolks, and eggs in a medium saucepan. Cook over medium, whisking constantly, until the mixture comes to a boil, about 5 minutes. Boil 1 minute, whisking constantly. Remove from heat, and whisk in the cold butter until incorporated.

3   Remove the shortbread crust from the refrigerator. Pour the lime curd evenly over the shortbread crust. Dot with the jam, and swirl with a wooden spoon or chopstick to create jam swirls.

4   Bake in the preheated oven until the filling is set, about 25 minutes. Cool in the pan on a wire rack to room temperature, about 1 hour. Cover and transfer to the refrigerator; chill until fully set, about 2 hours or overnight. Remove from the pan. Remove and discard foil, and cut into 24 bars.

BENNE SEED TUILE

The benne, or sesame, seed is a Southern favorite. Here it makes an appearance on dainty French tuiles, the cookies named for the curved terra-cotta roof tiles of France. These delicate cookies may be filled with whipped cream, meringue, or buttercream if you are so inclined.

MAKES 16 COOKIES **HANDS-ON** 20 MINUTES **TOTAL** 1 HOUR, 10 MINUTES

½   cup powdered sugar

⅓   cup cake flour

2   large egg whites, at room temperature

2   tablespoons white sesame seeds

2   tablespoons unsalted butter, melted

1   Preheat the oven to 350°F. Line a baking sheet with a silicone baking mat.

2   Beat all the ingredients in a medium bowl with an electric mixer on medium-high speed until smooth.

3   Place 1 tablespoon of the batter on the prepared baking sheet; using a small offset spatula, spread into a thin 3-inch-wide round. Repeat with the remaining batter to create 8 rounds, leaving 1 inch between the rounds. Bake in the preheated oven just until lightly browned around the edges, 8 to 9 minutes.

4   Let the cookies stand 1 minute. Using a small offset spatula, remove the cookies, and quickly roll each cookie loosely around the handle of a wooden spoon. Let stand until set, 3 to 5 minutes. Slide the cookies off the spoons, and cool completely on a wire rack, about 10 minutes. Repeat Steps 3 and 4 with the remaining batter.

JAMMY SHORTBREAD COOKIES

Consider these the jelly donuts of the cookie kingdom.

MAKES 3 DOZEN **HANDS-ON** 1 HOUR **TOTAL** 3 HOURS, 35 MINUTES, INCLUDING 2 HOURS CHILLING

½ cup unsalted butter, softened

3 ounces cream cheese, softened

2 tablespoons powdered sugar

½ teaspoon vanilla extract

½ teaspoon almond extract

1 cup all-purpose flour

¼ teaspoon kosher salt

¾ cup peach jam or other favorite jam

1 Beat butter and cream cheese with a heavy-duty electric stand mixer on medium speed until combined and whipped, about 30 seconds. Add powdered sugar, and beat until combined, about 30 seconds. Add vanilla and almond extracts, and beat until combined. Gradually add the flour and salt, beating on low speed until well blended. Shape the dough into a 4-inch disk. Wrap disk in plastic wrap; chill until firm, at least 2 hours.

2 Preheat the oven to 350°F. Place dough on a work surface heavily dusted with powdered sugar, and roll to ⅛-inch thickness. Using a 2½-inch round cutter, cut cookies from dough. Place on baking sheets lined with parchment paper. Chill until firm, about 10 minutes.

3 Spoon ½ teaspoon jam on each cookie. Fold opposite sides toward center of cookie, slightly overlapping edges and pressing firmly to adhere. (Powdered sugar should form a gluelike layer over cookie to help adhere.) Press down lightly on centers of cookies where dough overlaps.

4 Bake in preheated oven until lightly browned, 14 to 16 minutes. Cool on baking sheets on wire racks 5 minutes; transfer cookies to wire racks to cool completely, about 20 minutes.

LEMON-THYME-ROSEMARY
SCOOP-AND-BAKE TEA CAKES

A perfect pick-me-up for an afternoon slump, these delicious cookies are a nice treat for the office.

MAKES 5 DOZEN **HANDS-ON** 1 HOUR **TOTAL** 2 HOURS, 10 MINUTES, INCLUDING 1 HOUR CHILLING

1 cup unsalted butter, softened
2 cups granulated sugar
3 large eggs
2 teaspoons lemon zest (from 1 lemon)
1 teaspoon chopped fresh thyme
1 teaspoon chopped fresh rosemary
1 teaspoon vanilla extract
3½ cups all-purpose flour
1 teaspoon baking soda
½ teaspoon kosher salt

1 Beat the butter with a heavy-duty electric stand mixer on medium speed until creamy. Gradually add the sugar, beating until well combined. Add the eggs, 1 at a time, beating until blended after each addition. Add the lemon zest, thyme, rosemary, and vanilla, beating until blended. Stir together the flour, baking soda, and salt; gradually add the flour mixture to the butter mixture, beating at low speed until blended.

2 Divide the dough in half, and flatten each half into a disk. Wrap each disk in plastic wrap, and chill until cold, about 1 hour.

3 Preheat the oven to 350°F. Unwrap the disks, and scoop the dough into 1½-tablespoon-size balls. Place the dough balls 2 inches apart on parchment paper-lined baking sheets.

4 Bake in the preheated oven until the edges begin to brown, 10 to 12 minutes. Cool on baking sheets on wire racks 5 minutes; transfer the cookies to wire racks to cool completely, about 20 minutes.

HOLIDAY MENUS

FESTIVE FEAST

Kick off the holiday season this year with a family occasion sure to make a lasting impression. Trim the tree, deck the halls, and share in a festive feast that hits all the right notes.

THE MENU
Serves 6 to 8

Hot Mulled Fruit Punch

Santa's Sipper

Winter Panzanella

Roasted Cornish Game Hens with Shallots and Grapes

Shingled Butternut Squash with Brown Sugar and Coriander

Buttered Broccolini with Seared Citrus

Homemade Scottish Coffee

Pear-Chestnut Galette with Brown Butter-Caramel Sauce

Santa's Sipper

HOT MULLED FRUIT PUNCH

If Christmas had a flavor, it would be this punch—a take on the classic German Kinderpunsch, which mulls apple, cherry, and orange juices together with honey and hibiscus tea. This warm mocktail relies on cranberry in place of cherry and turns to Southern sorghum syrup instead of the usual honey. Photo page 199.

SERVES 8 **HANDS-ON** 10 MINUTES **TOTAL** 35 MINUTES

2 cups bottled not-from-concentrate orange juice

2 cups bottled apple juice

2 cups water

1 cup bottled cranberry juice

¼ cup thinly sliced fresh ginger (from a 2-inch piece)

3 (3-inch) cinnamon sticks, plus more for garnish

10 whole cloves

5 whole allspice berries

5 hibiscus tea bags or 5 teaspoons loose tea

½ cup sorghum syrup or dark molasses
Garnishes: orange slices, fresh cranberries, apples, cinnamon sticks (optional)

1 Bring the orange juice, apple juice, water, cranberry juice, ginger, cinnamon sticks, cloves, and allspice berries to a boil in a large saucepan over medium-high, stirring occasionally. Cover, reduce heat to medium, and simmer 15 minutes. Remove from the heat.

2 Add the tea bags, and steep 10 minutes. Remove, and discard the tea bags, squeezing out any excess liquid. Stir in the sorghum syrup until dissolved. Serve hot. Garnish, if desired.

SANTA'S SIPPER

This potent tipple is tailor-made for sipping by the holiday hearth. If you enjoy more than one, be sure to let the reindeer pull your sleigh.

SERVES 1 **HANDS-ON** 5 MINUTES **TOTAL** 5 MINUTES

1 orange peel twist

1 large ice cube or whiskey rock

¼ cup (2 ounces) bourbon, preferably overproof

1½ tablespoons (½ ounce) sweet vermouth (such as Carpano Antica Formula)

1½ teaspoons (¼ ounce) maraschino liqueur

2 teaspoons (¼ ounce) amaro liqueur

Rub the orange twist on rim of a coupe glass; place the twist and ice cube in the glass. Fill a cocktail shaker with ice or a whiskey rock; add the bourbon, vermouth, and liqueurs. Cover with the lid, and shake vigorously until thoroughly chilled, about 10 seconds. Strain into the prepared glass. Serve immediately.

Roasted Cornish Game Hens with Shallots and Grapes *recipe on page 120*

Shingled Butternut Squash with Brown Sugar and Coriander *recipe on page 121*

Buttered ... with Sear... *recipe on ...*

RED AND GREEN

Serving an elegant menu family style
sets an easy tone. A somewhat casually
dressed table completes the tablescape.
The look is fun and festive without
feeling formal.

WINTER PANZANELLA

This is a cool-season spin on the traditional summer bread salad. Sweet and bitter veggies offer a balance of flavor and pleasing textures. Try this as a main-dish salad topped with grilled beef, pork, or fish too. If you can't find rosemary-sea salt bread, any crusty loaf will do. Before roasting, add a teaspoon of chopped fresh rosemary to the olive oil mixture you used to toss the vegetables.

SERVES 6 **HANDS-ON** 20 MINUTES **TOTAL** 1 HOUR, 20 MINUTES

1 pound golden beets, peeled and cut into ¾-inch cubes (about 3 cups)

12 ounces Brussels sprouts, trimmed and halved (about 2¼ cups)

8 ounces parsnips, peeled and cut into ¾-inch pieces (about 1¼ cups)

1 medium-size red onion, cut into ¾-inch pieces (about 2 cups)

11 tablespoons olive oil

1½ teaspoons black pepper

1¼ teaspoons kosher salt

1 (1-pound) crusty rosemary-sea salt bread loaf, cut into 1-inch cubes (about 8 cups)

3 tablespoons sherry vinegar

1 tablespoon pure maple syrup

2 teaspoons whole-grain Dijon mustard

3 cups loosely packed chopped curly kale

6 ounces goat cheese, crumbled (about ¾ cup)

½ cup toasted pecans, coarsely chopped

1 Arrange the racks in the upper and bottom third of oven. Preheat the oven to 425°F. Toss together the beets, Brussels sprouts, parsnips, onion, and 2 tablespoons of the oil, ¾ teaspoon of the pepper, and ¾ teaspoon of the salt. Distribute between 2 large rimmed baking sheets, and bake in the preheated oven until browned and tender, about 30 minutes, stirring the vegetables and switching the pan placement halfway through. Remove from the oven, and cool completely, about 15 minutes.

2 Meanwhile, toss the bread with ¼ cup of the olive oil and ½ teaspoon of the pepper in a large bowl. Arrange in a single layer on a rimmed baking sheet, and bake at 425°F until golden brown and crisp, 10 to 12 minutes, stirring halfway through. Remove from the oven, and cool completely, about 10 minutes.

3 Whisk together the vinegar, maple syrup, mustard, and remaining ½ teaspoon salt and ¼ teaspoon pepper in a small bowl. Slowly drizzle in the remaining 5 tablespoons oil, whisking constantly, until smooth.

4 Place the kale in a large bowl; drizzle with 2 tablespoons of the olive oil mixture, and gently massage with hands until softened. Add the roasted vegetables, toasted bread cubes, goat cheese, and pecans. Toss with the remaining olive oil mixture, and serve immediately.

ROASTED CORNISH GAME HENS WITH SHALLOTS AND GRAPES

A salt-and-herb dry brine seasons the meat and helps develop the crispy exterior that comes with high-temperature roasting. The sauce gets great depth of flavor and a rich hue from the deglazing of the pan. Photo page 116.

SERVES 6 HANDS-ON 25 MINUTES **TOTAL** 9 HOURS, 10 MINUTES, INCLUDING 8 HOURS CHILLING

HENS

- 6 (1½- to 2-pound) Cornish hens
- 3 tablespoons kosher salt
- 1½ tablespoons granulated sugar
- 1 tablespoon fresh thyme leaves
- 2 teaspoons black pepper
- ¼ cup olive oil

SAUCE

- 1 (1-pound) bunch red seedless grapes, on stems
- 4 medium shallots, halved
- 5 thyme sprigs
- ½ cup dry white wine
- 2½ cups chicken broth
- ¼ cup Dijon mustard
- ¾ teaspoon black pepper
- 1 teaspoon kosher salt

1 Prepare the Hens: Pat the hens as dry as possible using paper towels. Tie the ends of the legs together with kitchen twine; tuck the wing tips under, and place on a cutting board lined with paper towels. Let stand at room temperature 10 minutes. Meanwhile, combine salt, sugar, thyme, and pepper in a small bowl. Rub the skins and cavities completely with the salt mixture. Chill, uncovered, 8 hours or overnight. Remove from the refrigerator, and let stand at room temperature about 30 minutes.

2 Preheat the oven to 450°F. Arrange the hens, breast sides up, on a rack in a rimmed baking sheet. Brush the hens with olive oil. Roast in the oven until the skin is a deep golden brown and a meat thermometer inserted in each breast registers 160°F, 45 to 50 minutes. Transfer the hens to a large platter, reserving drippings on the baking sheet. Tent the hens with foil, and let stand 30 minutes.

3 Prepare the Sauce: Remove the rack from the baking sheet, and place the grapes, shallots, and thyme sprigs in the reserved drippings. Gently stir until well coated. Return to the oven, and roast at 450°F until the grapes blister and the shallots soften, about 15 minutes. Transfer the grapes carefully to the platter with the hens, reserving the drippings on the baking sheet. Place the baking sheet on the stove top over medium-high, and add the wine to the reserved drippings. Bring to a boil, stirring often. Boil, stirring to loosen the browned bits from the bottom of the baking sheet, until the liquid is reduced by half, about 3 minutes. Pour the drippings mixture into a medium saucepan, and whisk in the broth, mustard, and pepper until blended and smooth. Bring to a boil, and cook, stirring often, until reduced to 2 cups, about 8 minutes. Remove and discard the thyme sprigs; stir in the salt. Serve the sauce with the hens and grapes.

SHINGLED BUTTERNUT SQUASH WITH BROWN SUGAR AND CORIANDER

Winter squash takes the place of the usual sweet potato in this cheeseless gratin that is sure to become a new favorite side. Photo page 116.

SERVES 6 **HANDS-ON** 15 MINUTES **TOTAL** 45 MINUTES

1 (2-pound) butternut squash, peeled, halved, and seeded
3 tablespoons salted butter, melted
2 teaspoons dark brown sugar
1 teaspoon coriander seeds, coarsely crushed
1 teaspoon kosher salt
½ teaspoon black pepper

Preheat the oven to 425°F. Cut each squash half crosswise into ½-inch-thick slices. Slide a large knife or ruler underneath slices, and transfer slices to a lightly greased 11×7-inch baking dish, adjusting as necessary so that slices overlap slightly. Drizzle the butter evenly over the squash slices, and sprinkle evenly with the brown sugar, crushed coriander seeds, salt, and pepper. Bake in preheated oven until tender and golden brown, about 30 minutes.

BUTTERED BROCCOLINI
WITH SEARED CITRUS

This hybrid of broccoli and a Chinese broccoli called gai lan has tiny florets and long stalks reminiscent of asparagus. Grilling citrus caramelizes the juices a bit to create a sweet-and-sour sauce that balances the pleasing bitterness of the Broccolini. Photo page 116.

SERVES 6 **HANDS-ON** 10 MINUTES **TOTAL** 20 MINUTES

2 pounds Broccolini, trimmed

3 tablespoons unsalted butter, cut into 4 pieces

1 small orange, cut into ⅛-inch-thick slices

1 small lemon, cut into ⅛-inch-thick slices

1 teaspoon kosher salt

1 teaspoon crushed red pepper

½ teaspoon black pepper

1 Cook the Broccolini in boiling salted water to cover, 3 to 5 minutes or until crisp-tender. Plunge into ice water to stop the cooking process. Drain, and pat dry.

2 Arrange the Broccolini, butter, and orange and lemon slices on a grill pan. Sprinkle with the salt, crushed red pepper, and black pepper. Grill, turning from time to time, until the Broccolini is tender and fruit slices are charred, about 8 minutes. Brush with pan drippings, and serve immediately.

HOMEMADE SCOTTISH COFFEE

Drambuie is a Scottish liqueur made from Scotch, honey, herbs, and spices. No need to buy a bottle when you can re-create the flavors at home. This warm tipple is a flavorful, smoky riff on the more common Irish coffee. Photo page 125.

SERVES 8 **HANDS-ON** 10 MINUTES **TOTAL** 30 MINUTES

DIY DRAMBUIE

½ cup honey
½ cup water
1 tablespoon fresh rosemary leaves
1 teaspoon lightly crushed fennel seeds
¾ cup (6 ounces) Scotch whisky

VANILLA-ORANGE WHIPPED CREAM

1½ cups heavy cream, chilled
1 teaspoon vanilla bean paste or vanilla extract
1 teaspoon orange zest (from 1 orange)

ADDITIONAL INGREDIENTS

8 cups hot brewed coffee
Garnish: orange peel twists (optional)

1 Prepare the DIY Drambuie: Cook the honey, water, rosemary, and fennel seeds in a small saucepan over medium, stirring occasionally, until mixture becomes a light syrup, about 5 minutes. Cool completely, about 30 minutes. Pour into a 1-pint jar with a tight-fitting lid, and add the Scotch whisky. Cover with lid, and shake to combine. Let steep at room temperature until completely cooled, about 20 minutes. Pour liquid through a fine-mesh strainer into an airtight container, discarding solids. Store in refrigerator up to 6 months.

2 Prepare the Vanilla-Orange Whipped Cream: Beat the cream, vanilla, and zest with an electric mixer on medium speed or by hand until medium peaks form. Refrigerate in an airtight container until ready to use.

3 Combine 1 cup hot brewed coffee and 2 tablespoons DIY Drambuie in each of 8 footed glass mugs. Top with 2 tablespoons Vanilla-Orange Whipped Cream, and, if desired, garnish each with an orange twist.

PEAR-CHESTNUT GALETTE WITH
BROWN BUTTER-CARAMEL SAUCE

Chestnuts roasted on an open fire can't hold a candle to this decadent dessert that pairs the favorite
holiday nut with cool-season pears and sweet caramel.

SERVES 6 HANDS-ON 30 MINUTES TOTAL 1 HOUR

SWEETENED CHESTNUT PUREE
- 1 (6.5-ounce) package peeled and steamed chestnuts (such as Melissa's)
- ¼ cup granulated sugar
- 1 cup heavy cream
- 1 teaspoon vanilla bean paste

DOUGH
- 2½ cups all-purpose flour, plus more for work surface
- 2 teaspoons granulated sugar
- 1 teaspoon kosher salt
- 1 cup unsalted butter, cut into ½-inch pieces
- ¼ to ⅓ cup ice water

BROWN BUTTER-CARAMEL SAUCE
- ½ cup unsalted butter
- 1¼ cups granulated sugar
- ¾ cup heavy cream
- ¼ teaspoon sea salt

ADDITIONAL INGREDIENTS
- 4 medium-size red Anjou pears, cored (about 2 pounds)
- 1 cup fresh cranberries
- 2 tablespoons unsalted butter, melted
- ¼ cup heavy cream
- 2 tablespoons turbinado sugar
  Vanilla ice cream (optional)

1 Prepare the Sweetened Chestnut Puree: Process the chestnuts, granulated sugar, and heavy cream in a food processor until chestnuts are finely chopped and mixture is smooth. Add the vanilla bean paste, and pulse until incorporated. Store in an airtight container in refrigerator up to 1 week.

2 Prepare the Dough: Pulse the flour, sugar, and salt in a food processor until combined. Add the butter, and pulse until the mixture resembles coarse meal, about 10 pulses. With processor running, add ¼ cup ice water in a slow, steady stream, pulsing until dough forms a ball and pulls away from sides of bowl (dough should not be wet or sticky). Add a bit more water, 1 teaspoon at a time, as needed. Flatten dough into an 8-inch disk, and wrap with plastic wrap. Chill until firm, at least 1 hour.

3 Meanwhile, prepare the Brown Butter-Caramel Sauce: Melt the butter in a small saucepan over medium-low. Increase heat to medium, and cook, swirling often, until mixture is beginning to brown and smell nutty, about 5 minutes. Pour into a bowl, and cool completely, about 30 minutes.

4 Add the granulated sugar to saucepan, and return to medium. Cook, stirring often, until the sugar is melted and turns a deep amber color, about 8 minutes. Stir in the cooled brown butter until smooth. Reduce heat to low, and slowly stir in the cream until smooth. Increase heat to medium-low, and cook, stirring constantly, until glossy, about 2 minutes. Stir in the salt. Remove from heat.

5 Remove Dough from refrigerator, and let stand, wrapped, at room temperature 15 minutes before rolling. Place a large rimmed sheet pan in a cold oven. Preheat oven to 425°F. Place a large piece of parchment paper on a work surface, and lightly dust with flour. Roll Dough into 14×12-inch oval (about ⅛ inch thick) on prepared parchment. Spread chilled Sweetened Chestnut Puree over Dough, leaving a 2-inch border around edges. Thinly slice pears lengthwise, and arrange slices on crust in 4 rows, overlapping slices slightly. Top evenly with the cranberries. Brush the fruit with melted butter. Fold edges of dough over pear slices, creating a border crust, overlapping where needed. Brush the crust with cream, and sprinkle with turbinado sugar. Use parchment to transfer galette to hot pizza stone.

6 Bake in preheated oven until golden brown and pears are tender, 30 to 35 minutes. Drizzle with Brown Butter-Caramel Sauce just before serving. Serve warm or at room temperature with additional Brown Butter-Caramel Sauce and, if desired, vanilla ice cream.

Homemade Scottish Coffee
recipe on page 123

**Pear-Chestnut Galette with
Brown Butter-Caramel Sauce**

NIBBLES & SIPS

Raise a glass to the best presents of all—the people you love—with a cocktail party gift exchange that lets you cross everyone off your list in one festive and flavorful swoop.

THE MENU
Serves 6 to 8

Red Grape and Pink Peppercorn Shrub Mocktail

Pimm's Cranberry Sparkler

Honey-Walnut Crackers

Lemon-Goat Cheese Straws

Salumi Board

Herbed White Bean Spread

Fig, Apricot, and Apple Mostarda

Creole Chilled Shrimp Cocktail

Mini Key Lime Curd Pies

Fire-Balls!

Lemon-Goat Cheese Straws
recipe on page 133

**Red Grape and Pink
Peppercorn Shrub Mocktail**
recipe on page 131

Honey-Walnut Crackers
recipe on page 132

Salumi Board *recipe on page 134*

Fig, Apricot, and Apple Mostarda
recipe on page 136

Herbed White Bean Spread
recipe on page 135

Pimm's Cranberry Sparkler

RED GRAPE AND PINK PEPPERCORN SHRUB MOCKTAIL

This mocktail is sweet, tangy, and bright like fresh grapes with a peppery kick. Make the shrub mixture several days ahead. The simple syrup and white balsamic vinegar help to balance the astringent flavor of the grape skins. If you want to make a spirited drink, add a jigger of gin to each glass. Photo page 128.

SERVES 8 **HANDS-ON** 10 MINUTES **TOTAL** 8 HOURS, 10 MINUTES, INCLUDING 8 HOURS CHILLING

2 cups water

1½ cups granulated sugar

¼ cup pink peppercorns, lightly crushed

2 pounds red seedless grapes (about 5 cups)

1 cup white balsamic vinegar

4 cups lemon-lime soft drink (such as Sprite), chilled

1 Combine the water, sugar, and pink peppercorns in a small saucepan; bring to a boil over medium-high. Cook, stirring until the sugar dissolves, about 1 minute. Remove from the heat.

2 Place the grapes in a large bowl; lightly crush with a potato masher. Pour the sugar mixture over the grapes. Cover and chill 8 hours or overnight.

3 Pour the mixture through a fine-mesh strainer into a bowl; discard the solids. Stir in the vinegar.

4 Pour about ½ cup of the shrub into each of 8 glasses; top each with about ½ cup soft drink. (Adjust the amount of shrub as desired.) Store any leftover shrub in an airtight container in refrigerator up to 2 weeks.

PIMM'S CRANBERRY SPARKLER

Colorful and festive, this holiday sipper is made with gin-based Pimm's, a British spirit flavored with herbs and citrus. It pairs beautifully with cranberry juice and a bright berry garnish.

SERVES 8 **HANDS-ON** 5 MINUTES **TOTAL** 5 MINUTES

4 cups cranberry juice cocktail, chilled

2 cups (16 ounces) Pimm's No. 1, chilled

1 cup (8 ounces) elderflower liqueur

1 (750-milliliter) bottle Prosecco, chilled

Fresh raspberries

Stir together the cranberry juice, Pimm's, and liqueur in a pitcher. Pour about ¾ cup of the mixture into each of 8 tall glasses filled with ice; top each with ⅓ cup of the Prosecco and 3 fresh raspberries. Serve immediately.

HONEY-WALNUT CRACKERS

Super easy to make with readily available pantry staples, these crackers have a light crispiness because of baking powder. Work with half of the dough at a time for ease. Just be sure to keep the other half chilled until you are ready to roll. Photo page 128.

MAKES 4 DOZEN **HANDS-ON** 20 MINUTES **TOTAL** 1 HOUR, 30 MINUTES

2¼ cups all-purpose flour, plus more for work surface

1 teaspoon table salt

½ teaspoon baking powder

¾ cup unsalted cold butter, cut into ½-inch-thick slices

1 cup finely chopped walnuts

2 tablespoons honey

1 large egg
Kosher salt for sprinkling

1 Place the flour, salt, and baking powder in the bowl of a heavy-duty electric stand mixer; beat at low speed until combined, about 30 seconds. Scatter the butter over the top of the flour mixture. Beat at low speed until the mixture is crumbly and resembles coarse sand, 2 minutes and 30 seconds to 3 minutes. Add the walnuts, and beat on low speed just until blended.

2 Whisk together the honey and egg in a small bowl, and add it to the flour mixture. Beat on low speed until a ball forms, about 30 seconds to 1 minute. Place the dough on a lightly floured work surface. Pat the dough into a 10×5-inch rectangle; fold the dough in half. Divide the dough in half, and pat each half into a 10×5-inch rectangle. Cover each half with plastic wrap, and chill 30 minutes.

3 Preheat the oven to 325°F. Working with half of the dough (leave the remaining half in the refrigerator), roll into a ¼-inch-thick rectangle on a lightly floured surface; trim the edges into straight sides. Cut the dough into 2-inch squares using a sharp knife. Sprinkle with salt.

4 Place the squares 1½ inches apart on parchment paper-lined baking sheets. Prick the center of each cracker with a fork. Bake in the preheated oven until golden brown, 14 to 16 minutes. Let stand on baking sheets 5 minutes; transfer to wire racks to cool. Repeat process with the remaining half of the dough.

LEMON-GOAT CHEESE STRAWS

A tasty nibble with a glass of wine, these cheese straws also make a delicious food gift.
Be certain to chill the dough for at least 45 minutes before baking in order to set the cheese.
Photo page 128.

MAKES 40 STRAWS **HANDS-ON** 20 MINUTES **TOTAL** 1 HOUR, 45 MINUTES

4   ounces goat cheese log, softened
4   ounces cream cheese, softened
2   tablespoons heavy cream
1   tablespoon lemon zest (from
    1 lemon)
1   (14-ounce) package frozen
    puff pastry sheet, thawed (such
    as Dufour)
    All-purpose flour, for work surface
1   large egg, lightly beaten
1   teaspoon kosher salt

1 Place the goat cheese, cream cheese, cream, and lemon zest in a bowl. Beat with an electric mixer on medium speed until smooth.

2 Roll the puff pastry sheet on a lightly floured surface into a 20×10-inch rectangle, about ⅛ inch thick.

3 Spread the goat cheese mixture on the bottom half of the pastry, leaving a ½-inch border around the edge. Brush the edges of the pastry with some of the egg. Fold the top half over the bottom half, enclosing the filling, making a 10- × 10-inch square; lightly press the edges of dough to seal. Sprinkle the salt evenly over the top of the dough; lightly pat the salt into the dough. Cut the dough in half lengthwise into 2 (10- × 5-inch) rectangles. Lightly press cut edges of the dough to seal. Brush the top of each rectangle with the remaining egg. Cut each rectangle into 20 (½- × 5-inch-wide) strips. Gently twist the strips and place 2 inches apart on baking sheets lined with parchment paper. Press the ends of the strips to adhere to the baking sheet (to keep from untwisting). Chill 45 minutes.

4 Preheat the oven to 375°F. Bake in the preheated oven until well browned, 18 to 22 minutes. Place the baking sheets on wire racks, and cool 5 minutes. Transfer the cheese straws to wire racks, and cool completely, about 20 minutes. Serve at room temperature.

SALUMI BOARD

Salumi boards are convenient for freeing up the host and allowing guests to graze on filling nibbles such as finely cured meats, tangy pickled vegetables, and crunchy breads. Don't avoid the pickled onions, which may be made up to a week ahead. They add a welcome tart element that cuts through the richness of many of the other components. The meats may be sliced the day before and kept well wrapped until serving time. Photo page 128.

SERVES 8 **HANDS-ON** 25 MINUTES **TOTAL** 8 HOURS, 25 MINUTES, INCLUDING 8 HOURS CHILLING

QUICK-PICKLED RED ONION

- ¾ cup white wine vinegar, distilled vinegar, or champagne vinegar
- ½ cup water
- ¼ cup granulated sugar
- ¼ teaspoon table salt
- ¼ teaspoon black pepper
- 1 large (about 12 ounces) red onion, cut into ¼-inch-thick slices (about 2½ cups)
- 1 small red Fresno chile, seeded and cut into rings (optional)

PROSCIUTTO-WRAPPED BREADSTICKS

- 1 (5.2-ounce) package shallot-and-chive spreadable cheese
- 1 (4.4-ounce) mini sesame breadsticks
- 8 thin slices prosciutto (about 2 ounces)

GARLICKY BAGUETTE

- 2 tablespoons olive oil
- 2 tablespoons salted butter, melted
- 1 garlic clove, grated
- 1 (12-ounce) baguette, cut into 20 (½-inch-thick) slices

ADDITIONAL INGREDIENTS

- 4 ounces soppressata, thinly sliced
- 4 ounces dry-cured Spanish chorizo, thinly sliced
- 4 ounces capicola, thinly sliced, folded into triangles
- 1 cup drained cornichons
- 3 ounces guava paste (such as La Cena)

1 Prepare the Quick-Pickled Red Onion: Combine the vinegar, water, sugar, salt, and black pepper in a saucepan; bring to a boil over medium-high, stirring until sugar is dissolved. Place the onion slices and, if desired, chile slices in a bowl; pour the vinegar mixture over the onion slices. Cover and let stand 8 hours or overnight. Drain just before serving.

2 Prepare the Prosciutto-Wrapped Breadsticks: Spread about 2 teaspoons cheese spread on each breadstick, leaving a 1-inch "handle." (Reserve the remaining cheese spread for another use.) Cut the prosciutto slices in half lengthwise. Wrap 1 slice of prosciutto around the cheese-covered end of each breadstick.

3 Prepare the Garlicky Baguette: Preheat the broiler with the oven rack 6 inches from the heat. Combine the oil, butter, and garlic in a small bowl. Arrange the baguette slices on a baking sheet, and brush with half of the oil mixture; broil until lightly toasted, about 1 minute. Remove the baking sheet from the oven. Turn the baguette slices over. Lightly brush the remaining oil mixture over the tops; broil until lightly toasted, about 1 minute.

4 To serve, arrange the Quick-Pickled Red Onion, Prosciutto-Wrapped Breadsticks, Garlicky Baguette, soppressata, chorizo, capicola, cornichons, and guava paste on a wooden serving board. Set out on a table for guests to serve themselves.

HERBED WHITE BEAN SPREAD

Creamy and earthy, this is both a delicious dip for vegetables and a tasty spread for crackers or sandwiches. Don't fear the anchovy paste. It adds a touch of umami complexity without being fishy or overpowering. Photo page 129.

SERVES 8 **HANDS-ON** 10 MINUTES **TOTAL** 1 HOUR, 10 MINUTES, INCLUDING 1 HOUR CHILLING

2 (15-ounce) cans white beans (such as cannellini), drained but not rinsed

3 tablespoons olive oil

2 tablespoons mayonnaise

2 tablespoons fresh lemon juice (from 1 lemon)

1½ teaspoons chopped fresh garlic

1 teaspoon table salt

¼ teaspoon black pepper

1 teaspoon anchovy paste (optional)

2 tablespoons chopped fresh flat-leaf parsley

2 tablespoons chopped fresh chives

1 tablespoon chopped fresh thyme

1 tablespoon chopped fresh tarragon

Process the beans, oil, mayonnaise, juice, garlic, salt, pepper, and, if desired, anchovy paste in a food processor until smooth, about 1 minute, stopping to scrape the sides of the bowl as necessary. Transfer the mixture to a bowl. Stir in the parsley, chives, thyme, and tarragon. Cover and chill 1 hour before serving.

FIG, APRICOT, AND APPLE MOSTARDA

Sweet fruit, pungent mustard, and tart vinegar are a harmonious blend in this cracker and cheese topper that's also a tasty accent for red meats. Don't boil the fruit too long at high heat or it will fall apart and become mushy. Just simmer gently, stirring occasionally, to keep it from sticking or scorching. Photo page 129.

MAKES ABOUT 3 CUPS **HANDS-ON** 15 MINUTES **TOTAL** 8 HOURS, 45 MINUTES, INCLUDING 8 HOURS CHILLING

2   cups chopped, peeled tart apples (such as Granny Smith) (from 2 large apples)
1   cup chopped dried figs
1   cup chopped dried apricots
1   cup cranberry juice cocktail (such as Ocean Spray)
½   cup water
¼   cup granulated sugar
2   teaspoons orange zest, plus 3 tablespoons fresh juice (from 1 orange)
¼   teaspoon kosher salt
1   tablespoon, plus 1 teaspoon mustard seeds
¼   cup white balsamic vinegar
1   tablespoon Dijon mustard
    Assorted crackers

1 Combine the apples, figs, apricots, cranberry juice, water, sugar, zest, orange juice, salt, and 1 tablespoon of the mustard seeds in a medium saucepan; bring to a boil over medium-high. Reduce heat to medium-low, and simmer until the fruit is very soft (but not falling apart) and the mixture just thickens, 30 to 35 minutes.

2 Transfer the mixture to a bowl; stir in the vinegar, Dijon, and remaining 1 teaspoon mustard seeds. Cover and chill 8 hours or overnight. Serve chilled or at room temperature with crackers.

CREOLE CHILLED SHRIMP COCKTAIL

This Creole sauce is chunkier than a typical shrimp cocktail, but it works well. Blend it if you prefer a more traditional texture. Prepare the sauce and shrimp the night before to make the day of the party a breeze. Photo page 211.

SERVES 8 **HANDS-ON** 25 MINUTES **TOTAL** 9 HOURS, 45 MINUTES, INCLUDING 8 HOURS CHILLING

2 tablespoons olive oil

2 (8-ounce) packages precut trinity mix (onion, celery, bell peppers)

6 garlic cloves, chopped

2 tablespoons tomato paste

2 (14½-ounce) cans diced tomatoes, undrained

2 teaspoons dried thyme

2 teaspoons dried oregano

1 teaspoon granulated sugar

4 teaspoons table salt

1 teaspoon crushed red pepper

2 teaspoons lemon zest, plus 2 tablespoons fresh juice (from 1 lemon)

2 teaspoons prepared horseradish

1½ teaspoons Creole seasoning

3 quarts water

1 cup white wine

1 lemon, cut into ½-inch-thick slices

2 pounds medium raw Royal Red shrimp

¼ cup torn fresh flat-leaf parsley leaves (optional)

Garnish: lemon slices (optional)

1 Heat the oil in a large skillet over medium-high. Add the trinity mix; cook, stirring occasionally, until tender, about 6 minutes. Add the garlic; cook, stirring often, until fragrant, about 1 minute. Stir in the tomato paste; cook, stirring often, until beginning to brown, about 2 minutes. Stir in the diced tomatoes, thyme, oregano, sugar, 2 teaspoons of the salt, and ½ teaspoon of the crushed red pepper; bring to a boil. Reduce heat to medium-low, and simmer, stirring often, until the mixture thickens, about 15 minutes. Stir in the lemon zest and juice, horseradish and Creole seasoning. Remove from heat and let cool 1 hour. Add the mixture to the bowl of a food processor and puree 1 minute. Transfer to a container, cover, and chill 8 hours or overnight.

2 Combine the water, wine, lemon slices, and the remaining 2 teaspoons salt and ½ teaspoon crushed red pepper in a Dutch oven; bring to a boil. Remove the Dutch oven from heat; stir in the shrimp. Cover and let stand until the shrimp are pink and just cooked through, 3 to 4 minutes. Drain and transfer the shrimp to a bowl filled with ice water until cold, about 10 minutes. Drain; peel, cover, and chill until ready to serve.

3 To serve, place the chilled Creole sauce in the center of a chilled glass. Place the shrimp around the rim of the glass. Garnish with the parsley and lemon slices, if desired, and serve immediately.

MINI KEY LIME CURD PIES

These little tartlets are sure to be inhaled, but if you are lucky to have a bit of extra lime curd, it keeps well in the refrigerator and can be used on biscuits, scones, and as a delicious topping for pound cake. You might consider making a double batch of curd to have a jar on hand in the fridge for just such purposes.

MAKES 5 DOZEN **HANDS-ON** 30 MINUTES **TOTAL** 8 HOURS, 30 MINUTES, INCLUDING 8 HOURS CHILLING

7   tablespoons unsalted butter

1½ cups granulated sugar

¾   cup Key lime juice (such as Nellie & Joe's)

4   large eggs

2   large egg yolks

1   tablespoon, plus ½ teaspoon lime zest (from 1 lime)

4   (1.9-ounce) packages prebaked frozen mini phyllo shells (such as Athens), thawed

1   cup heavy cream

¼   cup powdered sugar

¼   teaspoon vanilla extract
     Garnishes: mint sprigs, lime zest

1 Melt the butter in a large saucepan over medium-low; whisk in the sugar, juice, eggs, egg yolks, and 1 tablespoon of the zest. Cook, whisking constantly, until the mixture thickens and coats the back of a spoon, 14 to 16 minutes. (Do not boil.) If lumps have formed, pour through a fine-mesh strainer into a medium bowl, and discard the solids. Place plastic wrap directly on top of the filling to keep a film from forming. Chill until set, 8 to 12 hours.

2 Spoon the filling evenly into the mini shells.

3 Combine the cream, powdered sugar, and vanilla in a medium bowl. Beat with an electric mixer on high speed until medium peaks form. Spoon a dollop of whipped cream on each pie; top each with a mint sprig and a pinch of the zest.

FIRE-BALLS!

Fireball whisky spiked with spicy cinnamon adds kick to these sweet, creamy milk chocolate truffles.

MAKES 4 DOZEN **HANDS-ON** 20 MINUTES **TOTAL** 2 HOURS, 5 MINUTES

3   (4-ounce) Baker's German sweet chocolate baking bars, finely chopped

½   cup heavy cream

3   tablespoons light corn syrup

¼   cup (2 ounces) cinnamon-flavor whisky (such as Fireball)

½   teaspoon vanilla extract

1½ cups cinnamon graham cracker crumbs (from 12 to 14 sheets)

2   cups chopped toasted pecans

1 Place the chocolate, cream, and corn syrup in a medium-size microwavable bowl. Microwave on HIGH until the chocolate melts, about 1 minute, stirring every 20 seconds. Gently stir until smooth. Let stand 3 minutes.

2 Stir the whisky and vanilla into the chocolate mixture until smooth. Stir in the crumbs until coated. Cover and chill until the chocolate is firm enough to shape into balls, about 45 minutes.

3 Spread the chopped pecans in a shallow dish. Shape the chocolate mixture into 1-inch balls (about 2 teaspoons each), and roll in the chopped pecans. Place on waxed paper-lined baking sheets. Chill 1 hour. Store in an airtight container in the refrigerator up to 1 week.

Fire-Balls!

**Mini Key Lime
Curd Pies**

CHRISTMAS MORNING BRUNCH

Rise and shine! Greet loved ones on Christmas morning with a leisurely breakfast to share after presents are opened. Plenty of make-ahead options make pulling it together easy.

THE MENU
Serves 6 to 8

Holiday Yogurt Bar

Buttermilk Biscuit Sweet Rolls with Blueberry Filling

Bourbon-and-Pecan Bacon

Green Chile, Bacon, and Egg Casserole

Pomegranate-Gin Smash

Basic Chai

Russian Black Bread

Beet-and-Horseradish-Cured Gravlax

Benedictine Spread

Holiday Yogurt Bar
recipe on page 145

Green Chile, Bacon, and Egg Casserole
recipe on page 147

Buttermilk Biscuit Sweet Rolls with Blueberry Filling *recipe on page 146*

Bourbon-and-Pecan Bacon
recipe on page 147

Basic Chai *recipe
on page 148*

Holiday Yogurt Bar

HOLIDAY YOGURT BAR

The toppings here are as good with yogurt as they are on a dessert bar with ice cream.

SERVES 12 **HANDS-ON** 45 MINUTES **TOTAL** 45 MINUTES

¾ cup honey

1 vanilla bean, split

8 Bosc pears (about 2½ pounds), peeled and chopped

1 cup sweetened dried cranberries

½ cup granulated sugar

½ cup apple cider

2 tablespoons fresh lemon juice (from 1 lemon)

½ teaspoon ground cinnamon

8 cups plain whole-milk Greek yogurt

3 cups granola

1 cup toasted pecans

¾ cup roasted, salted pepitas (shelled pumpkin seeds)

¾ cup sweetened flaked dried coconut, toasted

1 tablespoon flaky sea salt

1 Place the honey in a small saucepan. Scrape the vanilla bean seeds into the honey in saucepan, and add the vanilla bean to the honey. Cook over medium-low, stirring often, until runny, about 6 minutes. Remove from the heat, and let cool at least 15 minutes. Remove and discard the vanilla bean.

2 While the honey cools, combine the pears, cranberries, sugar, cider, lemon juice, and cinnamon in a large saucepan over medium-low. Cover and cook, stirring occasionally, until the pears are just tender, about 25 minutes. Transfer the pear mixture to a serving bowl, and let cool until just warm, at least 15 minutes.

3 Place the yogurt, granola, pecans, pepitas, coconut, salt, and cooled honey mixture in separate serving bowls, and serve with the pear mixture. Let guests assemble their own combinations.

BUTTERMILK BISCUIT SWEET ROLLS WITH BLUEBERRY FILLING

Flaky buttermilk biscuits with blueberry filling are a Southerner's dream. Photo page 142.

SERVES 12 **HANDS-ON** 30 MINUTES **TOTAL** 1 HOUR, 30 MINUTES

- 2 cups fresh or frozen blueberries (about 10 ounces)
- 6 tablespoons granulated sugar
- 2 tablespoons water
- ⅛ teaspoon kosher salt
- ½ cup cold unsalted butter, cut into small cubes
- 2½ cups self-rising flour
- ¼ cup shortening, frozen and cut into small pieces, plus more shortening for greasing pan
- 1 tablespoon orange zest, plus 1 tablespoon fresh orange juice (from 1 large orange)
- 1 cup whole buttermilk
- 3 ounces cream cheese, softened
- 1½ teaspoons fresh lemon juice (from 1 lemon)
- 1¼ cups powdered sugar

1 Place 1½ cups of the blueberries and ¼ cup of the granulated sugar in a medium saucepan; stir in the water and salt, and bring to a simmer over medium. Cook, stirring often to mash the blueberries, until thickened, about 10 minutes. Transfer the mixture to a medium bowl; add ¼ cup of the butter and the remaining ½ cup blueberries, stirring until the butter melts. Cool completely, about 30 minutes.

2 Preheat the oven to 450°F. Stir together the flour and the remaining 2 tablespoons sugar in a large bowl. Cut in frozen shortening pieces and the remaining ¼ cup butter cubes with a pastry blender until the mixture is crumbly and resembles small peas. Stir in 2 teaspoons of the orange zest. Freeze 10 minutes.

3 Using a fork, stir the buttermilk into the flour mixture just until the dough comes together. (Dough will be very sticky and shaggy.) Turn the dough out onto a heavily floured surface, and knead 8 to 10 times. Transfer the dough to a heavily floured 18-inch-long piece of waxed paper or parchment paper. Roll the dough into a 14×10-inch rectangle. Gently spread the blueberry mixture over the dough, leaving a 1-inch border.

4 Lift and tilt the waxed paper, and roll up the dough, jelly-roll fashion, starting at 1 long side and using the waxed paper as a guide. Cut the dough into 14 (1-inch-thick) slices, discarding end slices. (You should have 12 rolls.) Grease a 9-inch round pan with shortening, and place the rolls in the prepared pan. Bake in the preheated oven until the rolls are golden brown and cooked through, 14 to 16 minutes. Cool in the pan on a wire rack 5 minutes.

5 Meanwhile, beat the cream cheese with an electric mixer on medium speed until creamy. Add the orange juice, lemon juice, and remaining 1 teaspoon orange zest, beating until smooth. Gradually add the powdered sugar, beating until smooth. Spoon the glaze over the warm rolls.

BOURBON-AND-PECAN BACON

A trio of Southern flavors collides in this breakfast favorite: bacon, bourbon, and pecans.
Photo page 143.

SERVES 12 **HANDS-ON** 10 MINUTES **TOTAL** 1 HOUR

⅓ cup pure maple syrup

2 tablespoons (1 ounce) bourbon

¾ teaspoon black pepper

½ cup pecan halves, finely chopped

12 thick-cut bacon slices (about 1 pound)

Preheat the oven to 350°F. Bring the maple syrup, bourbon, and pepper to a simmer in a small saucepan over medium. Remove from the heat, and stir in the pecans. Arrange the bacon in a single layer on a wire rack coated with cooking spray; place in an aluminum foil-lined rimmed baking sheet. Spread the pecan mixture evenly over the bacon slices. Bake in preheated oven until crisp, 40 to 45 minutes. Let cool at least 5 minutes before serving.

GREEN CHILE, BACON, AND EGG CASSEROLE

Incredibly savory and comforting, this breakfast casserole with a Southwestern flair is destined to become a new family favorite. Photo page 142.

SERVES 12 **HANDS-ON** 20 MINUTES **TOTAL** 1 HOUR, 15 MINUTES

6 thick-cut bacon slices (about 8 ounces)

10 large eggs, well beaten

1 (24-ounce) container cottage cheese

¼ cup all-purpose flour

1 teaspoon baking powder

¾ teaspoon kosher salt

6 ounces Monterey Jack cheese, shredded (about 1½ cups)

6 ounces sharp Cheddar cheese, shredded (about 1½ cups)

3 (4-ounce) cans chopped green chiles, drained
Hot sauce

1 Preheat the oven to 350°F. Cook the bacon in a large nonstick skillet over medium, turning occasionally, until crisp, 10 to 12 minutes. Transfer the bacon to a plate lined with paper towels to drain, reserving ¼ cup drippings; crumble the bacon.

2 Whisk together the eggs, cottage cheese, flour, baking powder, salt, and the reserved drippings in a large bowl. Stir in the cheeses, chiles, and crumbled bacon. Pour into a lightly greased 13×9-inch baking dish. Bake in the preheated oven until the middle is puffed and edges are light golden brown, 45 to 50 minutes. Let stand 10 minutes before serving. Cut into 12 pieces, and serve with hot sauce.

POMEGRANATE-GIN SMASH

This is a well-balanced but stiff cocktail. Pomegranate juice is a tart partner for the sweet honey syrup and bitter gin. Seltzer tops off this bubbly refresher. Photo page 151.

SERVES 12 **HANDS-ON** 15 MINUTES **TOTAL** 1 HOUR, 15 MINUTES

HONEY-GINGER SYRUP

¾ cup honey
½ cup water
2 tablespoons chopped fresh ginger (from 1 [1-inch] piece)
1½ teaspoons finely minced lime zest (from 1 lime)

COCKTAIL

3 cups pomegranate juice
3 cups (24 ounces) gin
⅓ cup fresh lemon juice (from 1 large and 2 medium lemons)
3 cups ice
2¼ cups seltzer water

1 Prepare the Honey-Ginger Syrup: Stir together all the syrup ingredients in a small saucepan. Bring to a boil over medium-high, stirring occasionally. Reduce the heat to medium-low, and simmer, stirring occasionally, until the honey is melted, about 2 minutes. Remove from the heat, and let cool to room temperature, about 1 hour. Pour the mixture through a fine-mesh strainer, discarding solids. Refrigerate the syrup in an airtight container until ready to use. Store in the refrigerator up to 2 weeks.

2 Prepare the Cocktail: Stir together the pomegranate juice, gin, Honey-Ginger Syrup, and lemon juice in a large pitcher. Add the ice, and stir well. Gently stir in the seltzer.

BASIC CHAI

As satisfying as the creamy spiced chai from your corner coffee shop. Photo page 143.

SERVES 12 **HANDS-ON** 5 MINUTES **TOTAL** 20 MINUTES

12 cardamom pods
16 whole cloves
1 teaspoon black peppercorns
12 cups water
4 (3-inch) cinnamon sticks
2 (1½-inch) pieces fresh ginger, thinly sliced
8 regular-size black tea bags (such as Darjeeling)
4 cups whole milk
1 cup granulated sugar
1½ cups (12 ounces) rum (optional)

1 Place the cardamom, cloves, and peppercorns in a small resealable plastic freezer bag. Crush with a heavy skillet.

2 Place the water, cinnamon sticks, and ginger in a medium saucepan; add the crushed spices from resealable bag, and bring to a boil over high. Reduce the heat to medium-low, and simmer 10 minutes. Remove from the heat. Add the tea bags; cover and steep 5 minutes. Discard the tea bags. Pour through a fine-mesh strainer into a pitcher or clean saucepan, discarding solids. Add the milk and sugar, stirring until sugar is dissolved. Pour into mugs, and, if desired, stir 2 tablespoons (1 ounce) rum into each serving.

RUSSIAN BLACK BREAD

This dense, sweet and slightly sour bread is a classic with gravlax. Its distinct color comes from the molasses, cocoa powder, and pumpernickel. Photo page 151.

SERVES 12 **HANDS-ON** 15 MINUTES **TOTAL** 5 HOURS, INCLUDING 1 HOUR RISING; 1 HOUR, 30 MINUTES STANDING; AND 1 HOUR COOLING

1¾ teaspoons active dry yeast (from 1 [2¼-ounce] envelope)

1 teaspoon granulated sugar

1 cup warm water (100°F to 110°F)

1 cup pumpernickel flour or dark rye flour

2 tablespoons unsweetened cocoa

1½ teaspoons caraway seeds

1¼ teaspoons kosher salt

1 teaspoon instant espresso granules

½ teaspoon fennel seeds

2½ cups bread flour

¼ cup unsalted butter, melted

2 tablespoons unsulfured molasses

1 Sprinkle the yeast and sugar over warm water in a small bowl; stir to combine. Let stand until foamy, 5 minutes.

2 Stir together the pumpernickel flour, cocoa, caraway seeds, salt, instant espresso, fennel seeds, and 1½ cups of the bread flour in a medium bowl.

3 Place the yeast mixture, butter, and molasses in the bowl of a stand mixer fitted with the dough hook. Beat on low speed, gradually adding the flour mixture until a sticky dough forms, about 2 minutes. Add the remaining 1 cup flour, ¼ cup at a time, until the dough pulls away from the sides of the bowl. Increase the speed to medium, and beat until smooth and elastic, 3 to 4 minutes. Transfer the dough to a lightly greased large bowl, turning to grease the top. Cover loosely with plastic wrap; let rise in a warm place (80°F to 85°F), free from drafts, until doubled in bulk, 1 to 1½ hours.

4 Punch the dough down to deflate. Shape into a 9-inch oblong loaf; transfer, seam side down, to a lightly greased 9×5-inch loaf pan. Cover loosely with lightly greased plastic wrap. Let stand in a warm place (80°F to 85°F), free from drafts, until doubled in bulk, 1½ hours.

5 Preheat the oven to 375°F. Cut a lengthwise slit, about ¼ inch deep, in the top of the loaf. Bake the bread until the crust is dry and deeply browned, 35 to 40 minutes. Remove the bread from the loaf pan to a wire rack to cool completely, 1 to 2 hours.

BEET-AND-HORSERADISH-CURED GRAVLAX

The color of this cured salmon is striking, but the flavor is something to rave about. The beets lend vibrant color and flavorful balance to the horseradish for a truly delightful spin on traditional gravlax.

SERVES 16 **HANDS-ON** 30 MINUTES **TOTAL** 4 DAYS, 30 MINUTES, INCLUDING 4 DAYS CHILLING

2 pounds red beets, peeled and quartered (from 6 medium beets)

4 ounces fresh horseradish, peeled and cut into chunks

½ cup kosher salt

⅓ cup granulated sugar

1 (1½- to 2-pound) center-cut, skin-on salmon fillet

10 (1-ounce) Russian Black Bread slices (page 149) or pumpernickel slices, toasted and cut into triangles
Benedictine Spread (recipe below)
Lemon zest
Chopped fresh dill

1 Position the shredding disc in a food processor bowl; pulse the beets in the food processor until grated to equal about 6 cups. Repeat with the horseradish, grating to equal ½ cup. Transfer the beets and horseradish to a large bowl, and stir in the salt and sugar until combined.

2 Cut the salmon in half crosswise. Line a large baking dish with plastic wrap, allowing 8 inches to extend on all sides. Place a thin layer of the mixture on the bottom of the dish; top with 1 salmon piece, skin side down. Spoon half of the remaining beet mixture over the salmon, and top with the remaining salmon piece, skin side up. Spoon the remaining beet mixture over the salmon. Pull plastic wrap tightly over the salmon to seal completely. Place a cast-iron skillet directly on top of the wrapped salmon. (Or use a large plate weighted with cans.)

3 Chill 24 hours. Remove the skillet or weighted plate, and turn the salmon over; drain, discarding liquid. Replace skillet or weighted plate, and chill 24 hours. Repeat process every 24 hours until the salmon is mostly firm, 3 to 4 days. (This process may take a day or 2 longer, depending on the thickness of the salmon.)

4 Remove the skillet or weighted plate and plastic wrap; discard plastic wrap. Drain and discard any liquid. Scrape off, and discard the beet mixture. Thinly slice the salmon; serve with the Russian Black Bread and the Benedictine Spread. Garnish with the lemon zest and dill.

BENEDICTINE SPREAD

This is a Kentucky Derby classic served with crackers at cocktail hour. The spread is named for caterer Jennie Carter Benedict, who spread it in the tea sandwiches she served in her Louisville, Kentucky, tea room. The spread may be made up to three days in advance and kept covered and chilled until ready to use. It's perfect with the Beet-and-Horseradish-Cured Gravlax.

MAKES 1 CUP **HANDS-ON** 10 MINUTES **TOTAL** 10 MINUTES

1 (8-ounce) package cream cheese, softened

1 cup finely diced English cucumber (from 1 small cucumber)

¼ cup finely chopped scallions (from about 2 medium scallions)

1 tablespoon mayonnaise

¼ teaspoon kosher salt

¼ teaspoon hot sauce

Combine the cream cheese, cucumber, scallions, mayonnaise, salt, and hot sauce in a medium bowl, and stir well.

Pomegranate-Gin Smash
recipe on page 148

Beet-and-Horseradish-Cured Gravlax
recipe on page 150

Russian Black Bread
recipe on page 149

CLASSIC SOUTHERN CHRISTMAS DINNER

Whether your family gathers on Christmas Eve or Christmas night to share in a meal of thanksgiving and celebration, this classic Southern menu is sure to keep them at the table.

THE MENU
Serves 6 to 8

Eggnog

Mocha Pecan Pralines

Southern Pecan Soup

Winter Greens Salad with Satsumas

Apple-Glazed Ham

Creamed Spinach with Toasty Breadcrumbs

Brown Butter-Garlic Mashed Potatoes

Roasted Rainbow Carrots with Orange Butter

Mulled Wine

Christmas Pudding with Brandy Sauce

Southern Pecan Soup
recipe on page 160

**Winter Greens Salad
with Satsumas** *recipe on page 161*

**Roasted Rainbow Carrots
with Orange Butter** *recipe on page 165*

**Brown Butter-Garlic
Mashed Potatoes**
recipe on page 164

Creamed Spinach with Toasty Breadcrumbs
recipe on page 163

Apple-Glazed Ham
recipe on page 162

Mocha
Pecan Pralines

Eggnog

comfort
& joy

EGGNOG

Eggnog is basically boozy crème anglaise. For a quick substitute, you could add cognac and rum to top-quality melted vanilla ice cream.

SERVES 16 **HANDS-ON** 1 HOUR **TOTAL** 10 HOURS, INCLUDING 8 HOURS CHILLING AND 1 HOUR COOLING

1½ cups granulated sugar
12 large eggs
6 cups whole milk
½ teaspoon kosher salt
4 cups heavy cream
½ cup (4 ounces) cognac
½ cup (4 ounces) dark rum
1 tablespoon vanilla extract
½ teaspoon ground nutmeg

1 Whisk together the sugar and eggs in a large glass bowl until well blended. Set aside.

2 Stir together the milk, salt, and 2 cups of the cream in a Dutch oven over medium-low. Cook, stirring occasionally, until the mixture begins to bubble around the edges of the Dutch oven (do not boil), about 15 minutes.

3 Gradually stir half of the hot milk mixture into the egg mixture. Gradually stir the egg mixture into the remaining hot milk mixture in the Dutch oven.

4 Cook the mixture over medium-low, stirring constantly, until the mixture slightly thickens and a thermometer inserted in the mixture registers 160°F, 25 to 30 minutes. Remove from the heat, and stir 1 minute. Pour the mixture through a fine-mesh strainer into a serving bowl. Stir in the cognac, rum, and vanilla; let cool 1 hour. Cover and chill 8 hours.

5 Beat the remaining 2 cups cream with an electric mixer on high speed until soft peaks form, about 1 minute. Fold the whipped cream into the chilled eggnog, and sprinkle with the nutmeg.

MOCHA PECAN PRALINES

This is a sophisticated and elegant take on the classic pecan praline. Espresso granules heighten the chocolate flavor without bitterness.

MAKES 2 DOZEN **HANDS-ON** 15 MINUTES **TOTAL** 1 HOUR, 15 MINUTES

3 cups packed light brown sugar
1 cup heavy cream
¼ cup light corn syrup
2 tablespoons salted butter
1 tablespoon instant espresso granules
2 ounces unsweetened chocolate baking squares
2 cups toasted pecan halves and pieces
1 teaspoon vanilla extract

1 Combine the brown sugar, cream, corn syrup, butter, and espresso in a heavy saucepan over medium. Bring to a boil, stirring occasionally, until a candy thermometer inserted in the mixture registers 236°F (soft ball stage), about 6 minutes. Remove the sugar mixture from the heat. Add the chocolate baking squares to the sugar mixture (do not stir).

2 Let the sugar mixture stand until a candy thermometer reaches 150°F, 30 to 35 minutes. Stir in the pecans and vanilla using a heatproof spoon or spatula. Using a tablespoon, quickly drop by heaping spoonfuls onto waxed or parchment paper; let stand until firm, 30 to 40 minutes.

SOUTHERN PECAN SOUP

Toasted pecans add a slightly bitter note that is balanced by the richness of cream and sweet onion.
Photo page 154.

SERVES 12 **HANDS-ON** 30 MINUTES **TOTAL** 2 HOURS, 30 MINUTES

3 tablespoons salted butter
2 cups chopped sweet onion (from 1 large onion)
½ cup chopped celery (from 2 stalks)
2 teaspoons minced garlic (from 2 garlic cloves)
3 cups coarsely chopped toasted pecans
4 cups chicken broth
4 thyme sprigs
1 bay leaf
1 teaspoon kosher salt
½ teaspoon black pepper
2 cups heavy cream
¼ cup chopped scallions (from 1 large scallion)

1 Melt the butter in a large saucepan over medium-high; add the onion and celery, and cook, stirring often, until softened, about 7 minutes. Stir in the garlic and 2½ cups of the pecans; cook until fragrant, 1 to 2 minutes. Stir in the broth, thyme sprigs, bay leaf, salt, and pepper, and bring to a boil. Cover, and reduce the heat to low; simmer, stirring occasionally until the pecans are very soft, about 2 hours.

2 Remove from the heat. Remove and discard the thyme sprigs and bay leaf; let stand 15 minutes. Transfer the soup to a high-powered blender. Remove the center piece of the blender lid (to allow the steam to escape); secure the lid on the blender, and place a clean towel over the opening in the lid. Process until smooth, about 1 minute. Return the mixture to the pan, and stir in the heavy cream. Reheat the soup, if necessary; garnish with the chopped scallions and remaining ½ cup pecans.

WINTER GREENS SALAD
WITH SATSUMAS

A bowl of verdant and varying textures brimming with flavor is always a crowd-pleaser. Be sure to toss the greens and onion together with a bit of the dressing and then add the toppings just before serving. Pass the remaining vinaigrette at the table. Photo page 155.

SERVES 12 **HANDS-ON** 20 MINUTES **TOTAL** 20 MINUTES

¼ cup apple cider vinegar

1 tablespoon grated fresh ginger

1 tablespoon honey

2 teaspoons Creole mustard

1 teaspoon kosher salt

½ teaspoon black pepper

½ cup olive oil

1 (5-ounce) package baby arugula

1 head butter lettuce, torn into bite-size pieces (about 4 cups)

1 romaine lettuce heart, torn into bite-size pieces (about 4 cups)

1 head radicchio, torn into bite-size pieces (about 4 cups)

½ cup thinly sliced red onion (from 1 small red onion)

4 satsumas or clementines, peeled and sectioned

1 (4-ounce) goat cheese log, crumbled

½ cup toasted slivered almonds

½ cup pomegranate arils

1 Whisk together the vinegar, ginger, honey, mustard, salt, and pepper in a small bowl. Slowly pour in the olive oil, whisking constantly until well blended.

2 Combine the arugula, butter lettuce, romaine, radicchio, onion, and ½ cup of the vinaigrette in a large bowl; toss to coat. Transfer to a large platter; top evenly with the satsumas and the goat cheese. Sprinkle with the almonds and pomegranate arils. Serve the remaining vinaigrette on the side.

APPLE-GLAZED HAM

Salty ham is a perfect match for the sweetness of apple and the tang of mustard. This lovely glazed version is an impressive centerpiece for company. Photo page 157.

SERVES 12 **HANDS-ON** 30 MINUTES **TOTAL** 2 HOURS, 20 MINUTES

1 (8- to 9-pound) bone-in, fully cooked smoked ham
1 tablespoon whole cloves
2½ cups apple cider
1 cup apple jelly
⅓ cup spicy brown mustard
¼ teaspoon apple pie spice

1 Place the ham, cut side down, in a large baking pan lined with heavy-duty aluminum foil lightly greased (with cooking spray); let stand at room temperature 30 minutes.

2 Preheat the oven to 350°F. Trim the rind or excess fat from the ham with a sharp knife. Score the outside of the ham with a knife in a decorative diamond pattern, without cutting through to the meat. Insert a whole clove into the center of each diamond. Cover the pan and ham with heavy-duty aluminum foil. Bake until a meat thermometer inserted in the ham registers 140°F, 1½ to 2 hours.

3 Bring the apple cider to a boil in a saucepan over medium-high, and cook until reduced to 1 cup, 15 to 20 minutes. Reduce the heat to medium. Add apple jelly, mustard, and apple pie spice, and cook, stirring constantly, until syrupy, about 5 minutes. Remove from heat.

4 Remove foil cover, and brush warm glaze over ham. Return ham to oven, uncovered, and roast until glossy and well browned, about 20 minutes, basting with remaining glaze every 10 minutes.

5 Remove ham from oven; tent loosely with aluminum foil to keep warm. Let stand 30 minutes before serving.

CREAMED SPINACH WITH TOASTY BREADCRUMBS

A heap of healthy greens and cream sauce—this is comfort food you can almost feel good about!

Photo page 157.

SERVES 12 **HANDS-ON** 45 MINUTES **TOTAL** 1 HOUR

3   tablespoons salted butter

2   tablespoons olive oil

1   cup chopped sweet onion (from 1 onion)

1   tablespoon, plus 1 teaspoon minced garlic (from 3 large cloves)

2   tablespoons all-purpose flour

1   cup half-and-half

4   ounces cream cheese, softened

1   cup (4 ounces) Parmesan cheese, grated

¾   teaspoon kosher salt

2   pounds baby spinach

1   cup panko (Japanese-style breadcrumbs)

2   tablespoons chopped slivered almonds

1 Preheat the oven to 425°F. Heat 1 tablespoon each butter and olive oil in a medium saucepan over medium-high. Add the onion and 1 tablespoon of the garlic; cook, stirring often, until tender and starting to turn golden, 4 to 5 minutes. Add the flour, and cook, stirring constantly, 1 minute. Stir in the half-and-half; reduce heat to medium, and simmer, stirring constantly, until thickened, about 2 minutes. Remove from the heat; stir in the cream cheese, Parmesan, and ½ teaspoon of the salt. Continue to stir until cheeses are melted and mixture is smooth.

2 Heat the remaining 1 tablespoon olive oil in a Dutch oven over medium. Add the spinach in batches; cover and cook until starting to wilt, 2 minutes. Toss with tongs until wilted, about 1 minute. Transfer the cooked spinach to a colander, and drain. Place the drained spinach in a kitchen towel, and squeeze dry. Coarsely chop the spinach. Place the spinach back in the Dutch oven.

3 Add the half-and-half mixture to the spinach; stir to combine. Transfer the mixture to a lightly greased (with cooking spray) 11×7-inch baking dish.

4 Place the remaining 2 tablespoons of butter and the 1 teaspoon garlic in a small microwavable bowl. Microwave on HIGH 30 seconds. Stir in the panko, almonds, and remaining ¼ teaspoon salt. Sprinkle the mixture evenly over the spinach mixture.

5 Bake in preheated oven until golden brown and bubbly, about 15 minutes.

BROWN BUTTER-GARLIC
MASHED POTATOES

Browning butter creates a nutty richness that starchy vegetables like potatoes soak up with magical results. Photo page 156.

SERVES 12 **HANDS-ON** 30 MINUTES **TOTAL** 40 MINUTES

2   pounds russet potatoes, peeled
     and cut into 2-inch cubes
2   pounds Yukon Gold potatoes,
     peeled and cut into 2-inch cubes
4   garlic cloves
1   tablespoon table salt
¾   cup salted butter
½   cup whole buttermilk
¼   cup whole milk
½   teaspoon black pepper
2   to 3 tablespoons chopped
     fresh chives

1   Combine the potatoes, garlic, 2 teaspoons of the salt, and water to cover in a large Dutch oven over medium-high; bring to a boil. Reduce the heat to medium, and simmer until the potatoes are very tender, 15 to 20 minutes. Drain. Reduce the heat to medium-low. Return the potatoes to the Dutch oven, and cook, stirring occasionally, until the potatoes are dry, 3 to 5 minutes.

2   Cook the butter in a 2-quart heavy saucepan over medium, stirring constantly, until the butter begins to turn golden brown, 6 to 8 minutes. Immediately remove the pan from the heat, and pour the butter into a small bowl. (Butter will continue to darken if left in saucepan.) Reserve 2 tablespoons of the brown butter for serving.

3   Mash the potatoes and garlic with a potato masher to desired consistency. Stir in the brown butter, buttermilk, milk, pepper, and remaining 1 teaspoon salt, stirring just until blended.

4   Transfer to a serving dish. Drizzle with the reserved brown butter, and sprinkle with chives.

ROASTED RAINBOW CARROTS
WITH ORANGE BUTTER

Orange and rosemary are a harmonious flavor match for sweet caramelized carrots in this colorful side dish for the holidays. Change it up with lemon and thyme or even lime and basil—just add the basil after roasting. Photo page 156.

SERVES 12 **HANDS-ON** 15 MINUTES **TOTAL** 1 HOUR

3   tablespoons salted butter,
      softened
2   teaspoons orange zest, plus
      1 teaspoon fresh juice (from
      1 orange)
½   teaspoon black pepper
1½ teaspoons kosher salt
3   pounds large rainbow carrots,
      peeled and cut diagonally into
      2-inch pieces
2   tablespoons olive oil
1   tablespoon chopped
      fresh rosemary

1   Preheat the oven to 450°F. Stir together the butter, orange zest, orange juice, pepper, and ¼ teaspoon of the salt in a small bowl; set aside.

2   Place the carrots on a large rimmed baking sheet; toss with the oil, rosemary, and the remaining 1¼ teaspoons salt. Spread in an even layer, and roast in the preheated oven 20 minutes, stirring once. Reduce the heat to 325°F, and bake, stirring occasionally, until the carrots are browned and tender, 20 to 25 minutes more.

3   Place the carrots and the butter mixture in a large bowl, and gently toss to coat. Serve immediately.

MULLED WINE

Soul-warming fortification for a night of caroling or snuggling by the fire, mulled wine is traditionally red wine that is steeped with spices and aromatics and sometimes spiked with additional spirits like brandy or cognac.

SERVES 12 **HANDS-ON** 5 MINUTES **TOTAL** 20 MINUTES

2   (750-milliliter) bottles red wine (such as red Zinfandel, Syrah, or Malbec)
4   cups apple cider
1¼ cups granulated sugar
1   tablespoon whole allspice
1½ teaspoons whole cloves
4   (3-inch) cinnamon sticks
3   whole star anise
2   medium oranges, thinly sliced, plus more for garnish

1   Combine all ingredients in a Dutch oven over medium, and bring to a boil. Reduce the heat to medium-low, and simmer until the flavors have melded, about 15 minutes.

2   Pour the mixture through a fine-mesh strainer into a pitcher or serving bowl, discarding the spices. Top individual servings with orange slices, or float on top of mulled wine in a serving bowl. Serve hot.

MULLING SPICE GIFT

Fill sachets, or a pretty tin that includes a tea diffuser, with mulling spice blend to give as a soothing gift for steeping with black tea, hot cider, or wine. Add a sachet or two to a pot of barely simmering water on the stove top to add a terrific holiday scent to your home.

Mulling Spice Sachets: Place 8 black peppercorns, 6 whole allspice, 6 whole cloves, 2 (3-inch) cinnamon sticks, and 3 (3×1-inch) orange zest strips on a 5-inch square of cheesecloth. Gather the edges, and tie securely with kitchen string.

CHRISTMAS PUDDING WITH BRANDY SAUCE

Originally, Christmas plum pudding was a porridge comprised of fruit, wine, and beef or mutton. Thankfully, it morphed over time into the more traditional, comforting egg-and-spice pudding dotted with dried fruit that we've come to know and love today.

SERVES 12 **HANDS-ON** 40 MINUTES **TOTAL** 3 HOURS, 40 MINUTES, INCLUDING BRANDY SAUCE

½ cup salted butter, softened

1 cup packed light brown sugar

1 tablespoon lemon zest (from 1 lemon)

4 large eggs

2½ cups all-purpose flour

1 teaspoon baking soda

1 teaspoon ground cinnamon

¼ teaspoon table salt

¼ teaspoon ground ginger

¼ teaspoon ground cloves

½ cup sour cream

1½ cups chopped dried figs (about 7½ ounces)

Brandy Sauce (recipe below)

1 Beat the butter with a heavy-duty electric stand mixer on medium speed until creamy; add the brown sugar, and beat until fluffy, about 1 minute. Add the lemon zest, and beat until combined. Add the eggs, 1 at a time, beating well after each addition.

2 Place 2 cups of the flour in a bowl; stir in the baking soda, cinnamon, salt, ginger, and cloves. Add to the creamed mixture alternately with the sour cream, beginning and ending with the flour mixture. Dredge the figs in the remaining ½ cup flour, and fold into the batter; discard excess flour. Spoon the batter into a well-greased (with shortening) 1½-quart steamed pudding mold, and cover tightly with the lid.

3 Place the mold on a wire rack set in a large stockpot; add enough boiling water to come halfway up the sides of the mold. Cover the stockpot; return the water to a boil over medium-high. Reduce the heat to low, and simmer 2½ to 3 hours. Remove the mold from the water, and cool slightly, about 10 minutes. Loosen the pudding from the sides of the mold. Unmold onto a serving plate. Poke holes with a skewer over the top of the pudding; pour the Brandy Sauce over the cooked pudding.

BRANDY SAUCE

MAKES ABOUT 1¼ CUPS **HANDS-ON** 18 MINUTES **TOTAL** 18 MINUTES

½ cup granulated sugar

1 tablespoon heavy cream

1 large egg

⅛ teaspoon table salt

½ cup salted butter, chilled, cut into ½-inch pieces

¼ cup (2 ounces) brandy

1 Pour water to a depth of 2 inches into bottom of a saucepan or double boiler; bring to a simmer over medium.

2 Combine the sugar, cream, egg, and salt in a heatproof bowl or top of double boiler; whisk constantly until pale yellow, about 2 minutes.

3 Place the bowl over simmering water. Gradually add the butter, 1 piece at a time, whisking to melt each before adding another. Cook, whisking constantly, until the sauce thickens, about 12 minutes. Remove from the heat, and stir in the brandy. Serve immediately.

Note: The pudding can also be made in a 1½- or 2-quart heatproof glass bowl covered tightly with heavy-duty aluminum foil.

SOUTHERN-STYLE NEW YEAR

Welcome in the New Year Southern style with good-luck fixin's—collards, black-eyed peas, hoppin' John, and plenty of pork and fried goodness to round out the menu.

THE MENU
Serves 6 to 8

Cajun Boiled Peanuts

Pickled Peppers and Onions

Braised Collard Greens with Caramelized Onions
and Toasted Fennel Seeds

Pear and Lemon-Lime Ale

Three-Pea Hoppin' John

Buttermilk-Brined Fried Chicken Drumettes
with Bacon-Honey Mustard Sauce

Crispy Spice-Rubbed Pork Belly Bites

Cornbread-and-Leek Pudding
with Parmesan

Braised Collard Greens with Caramelized Onions and Toasted Fennel Seeds *recipe on page 177*

Buttermilk-Brined Fried Chicken Drumettes with Bacon-Honey Mustard Sauce *recipe on page 181*

Pickled Peppers and Onions *recipe on page 176*

Crispy Spice-Rubbed Pork Belly Bites *recipe on page 182*

**Three-Pea Hoppin'
John** *recipe on
page 180*

**Cornbread-and-Leek
Pudding with Parmesan**
recipe on page 183

CAJUN BOILED PEANUTS

Be sure to buy peanuts in their shells. You can find liquid crab boil in the spice section of most supermarkets. Store the peanuts in the liquid and reheat to boiling before serving.

SERVES 24 **HANDS-ON** 15 MINUTES **TOTAL** 15 HOURS, 15 MINUTES, INCLUDING 8 HOURS SOAKING AND 1 HOUR STANDING

1 cup Cajun seasoning

3 pounds dried raw peanuts in the shell

½ cup kosher salt

1 (4-ounce) bottle liquid Cajun crab boil

1 Place ¾ cup of the Cajun seasoning in a large stockpot; add the peanuts and enough water to cover. Soak the peanuts at least 8 hours or up to 24 hours. (You may need to weight down the peanuts with a large plate or lid to ensure that they are fully submerged.) Drain and rinse.

2 Combine the peanuts, salt, crab boil, and remaining ¼ cup Cajun seasoning in a stockpot, and add water to cover. Bring to a boil over high; cover, reduce heat to medium-low, and simmer, stirring occasionally, until peanuts are tender, about 6 hours, adding water as needed to keep peanuts covered.

3 Remove from the heat, and let stand at room temperature 1 hour; serve warm with the cooking liquid.

PICKLED PEPPERS AND ONIONS

Serve these zesty pickled vegetables atop braised collards as you would chowchow or as part of a cheese and meat spread for appetizers. Pouring the vinegar brine over the vegetables while it's piping hot helps to pickle them faster. Photo page 172.

SERVES 8 HANDS-ON 10 MINUTES **TOTAL** 25 HOURS, 10 MINUTES, INCLUDING 24 HOURS CHILLING

½   small red onion, cut into ¼-inch-thick slices
    Ice water
½   red bell pepper, cut lengthwise into ¼-inch-wide strips
½   yellow bell pepper, cut lengthwise into ¼-inch-wide strips
½   green bell pepper, cut lengthwise into ¼-inch-wide strips
4   scallions, thinly sliced diagonally
1   cup apple cider vinegar
6   tablespoons granulated sugar
2   tablespoons kosher salt
½   teaspoon crushed red pepper
1   cup water

1 Soak the onion slices in ice water to cover in a small bowl 10 minutes; drain. Pack the onion slices, bell pepper strips, and scallions into a 1-quart canning jar.

2 Bring the vinegar, sugar, salt, red pepper, and 1 cup water to a boil in a small nonaluminum saucepan over medium-high, stirring occasionally until the sugar is dissolved.

3 Pour the hot vinegar mixture over the vegetables in the jar. Let stand, uncovered, 1 hour. Seal the jar, and chill 24 hours before serving. Store in the refrigerator up to 1 week.

BRAISED COLLARD GREENS WITH CARAMELIZED ONIONS AND TOASTED FENNEL SEEDS

Slow-cooked collards are a Southern staple that has long symbolized prosperity in the New Year because they are the same color as currency. Removing the caramelized onions at the end of Step 1 and then returning them to the dish at the end keeps the braising liquid from getting cloudy. Photo page 172.

SERVES 6 **HANDS-ON** 53 MINUTES **TOTAL** 3 HOURS

2   tablespoons olive oil
1   tablespoon unsalted butter
4   cups chopped yellow onions (from 3 medium onions)
3   garlic cloves, minced
3   cups low-sodium chicken broth
1   pound fresh collard greens, stems removed and leaves chopped
¼   cup apple cider vinegar
1½ teaspoons kosher salt
1   teaspoon black pepper
1   teaspoon toasted ground fennel seeds
    Hot sauce (optional)

1 Heat the oil and butter in a large Dutch oven over medium. Add the chopped onions; cook, stirring occasionally, 8 minutes. Reduce the heat to medium-low; cook, stirring occasionally, until light amber in color, about 45 minutes. Transfer the caramelized onions to a small bowl, and set aside.

2 Return the Dutch oven to medium. Add the garlic, and cook, stirring constantly, 1 minute. Stir in the chicken broth. Increase heat to high, and bring to a boil. Stir in the collard greens and vinegar. Reduce the heat to medium-low; cover and simmer, stirring occasionally, until the greens reach desired tenderness, about 2 hours.

3 Stir in the salt, pepper, ground fennel seeds, and caramelized onions. Serve with the hot sauce, if desired.

Pear and Lemon-Lime Soda

PEAR AND LEMON-LIME ALE

*This drink has a hint of ginger's essence and plenty of lemon-lime flavor that goes well with pear.
Be sure to add the ginger beer just before serving to maintain this mocktail's fizziness.*

SERVES 6 **HANDS-ON** 5 MINUTES **TOTAL** 5 MINUTES

4 cups pear nectar

3 cups chilled apple juice

2 tablespoons honey

2 tablespoons fresh lime juice (from 1 lime)

2 tablespoons fresh lemon juice (from 1 lemon)

2 (12-ounce) bottles ginger beer
Lime and lemon wheels

Combine the pear nectar, apple juice, honey, and lime and lemon juices in a punch bowl. Chill until ready to serve. Gently stir in the ginger beer, and serve immediately over ice. Garnish each serving with the lime and lemon wheels.

STOCKING A BAR

A basic bar should include liquor and mixers for what your guests, family, and friends prefer. Scotch, vodka, bourbon, gin, rum, and tequila are good bets. Stock lots of fruit juices and sparkling water for mixing and for nondrinkers.

To calculate how much to purchase, consider the number of guests, how long the party will last, and what other beverages will be served.

For each guest, estimate one drink, one beer, or two glasses of wine per hour. For those who don't consume alcoholic beverages, figure in three to four cans of cola or bottles of water for the party duration.

It's a best estimate when it comes to how much liquor, beer, or wine you'll need, so err on the side of caution by buying too much rather than too little. When purchasing liquor, ask if the store accepts returns of unopened bottles.

Use this guideline to help gauge what is needed for your party:

• 1 (750-milliliter) bottle liquor = 17 (1½-ounce) jiggers

• 1 (33.8-ounce) bottle liquor = 22 (1½-ounce) jiggers

• 1 (750-milliliter) bottle wine or Champagne = 6 (4-ounce) servings

THREE-PEA HOPPIN' JOHN

This dish of black-eyed peas, also called cowpeas, is eaten in the South on New Year's Day because it is believed to bring good luck all year. It is almost always served with collard greens and cornbread. Photo page 173.

SERVES 6 **HANDS-ON** 25 MINUTES **TOTAL** 3 HOURS, 45 MINUTES

8 ounces dried or frozen field peas

4 ounces dried or frozen crowder peas

4 ounces dried or frozen black-eyed peas

3 bay leaves

2 rosemary sprigs

3 thyme sprigs

3 whole garlic cloves, plus 2 minced garlic cloves

4 thick-cut bacon slices, chopped (about 6 ounces)

2 (8-ounce) smoked ham hocks

1 cup finely chopped sweet onion (from 1 medium onion)

9½ cups water

2 cups uncooked long-grain rice

3 teaspoons kosher salt

1 teaspoon black pepper

2 tablespoons chopped fresh flat-leaf parsley

1 Place all the peas in a Dutch oven; add water to cover the peas by 2 inches. Bring to a boil over high, and boil 1 minute. Cover, remove from the heat, and let stand at room temperature 1 hour. Drain the peas.

2 Meanwhile, place the bay leaves, rosemary, thyme, and 3 whole garlic cloves in the center of a 6-inch square of cheesecloth; tie with kitchen twine. Set garlic-and-herb bag aside.

3 Cook the chopped bacon in Dutch oven over medium-low, stirring occasionally, until crisp, about 10 minutes. Using a slotted spoon, transfer the bacon to paper towels to drain, reserving drippings in the Dutch oven.

4 Add the ham hocks to reserved drippings in the Dutch oven, and cook over medium-high, stirring occasionally, until the skin becomes crispy and lean portions of ham hocks are tender, about 5 minutes. Add the onion and remaining 2 minced garlic cloves; cook, stirring often, until the onion is translucent, about 2 minutes. Add the peas, garlic-and-herb bag, and 6 cups of the water. Bring to a boil over high, reduce the heat to medium, and simmer until the cooking liquid is rich and flavorful and the peas are tender, about 2 hours.

5 Meanwhile, bring the remaining 3½ cups water to a boil in a medium saucepan over high; stir in the rice and 2 teaspoons of the salt. Cover, reduce the heat to low, and simmer until the liquid is absorbed, about 15 minutes.

6 Remove and discard the ham hocks and garlic-and-herb bag from the Dutch oven. Season the pea mixture with pepper and the remaining 1 teaspoon salt. Pour the pea mixture through a fine-mesh strainer, reserving the cooking liquid and the peas separately.

7 Place the cooked rice and the drained peas in the Dutch oven, and cook over medium-low, stirring in the reserved cooking liquid, 1 cup at a time, until the mixture just binds together, about 5 minutes. Sprinkle each serving evenly with the chopped bacon and the chopped fresh parsley, and serve hot.

BUTTERMILK-BRINED FRIED CHICKEN DRUMETTES WITH BACON-HONEY MUSTARD SAUCE

Hot, crispy, crunchy fried chicken with a dipping sauce that perfectly cuts through all that yummy richness—this one's hard to beat! Photo page 172.

SERVES 6 **HANDS-ON** 20 MINUTES **TOTAL** 8 HOURS, 20 MINUTES, INCLUDING 8 HOURS CHILLING

1½ cups whole buttermilk
2 teaspoons kosher salt
3 tablespoons hot sauce
2½ pounds chicken drumettes
1 cup all-purpose flour
¾ teaspoon black pepper
¼ teaspoon onion powder
4 thick-cut bacon slices (about 6 ounces)
   Vegetable oil
6 tablespoons mayonnaise
3 tablespoons Dijon mustard
2 tablespoons honey
1 tablespoon white wine vinegar

1 Whisk together the buttermilk, salt, and 2 tablespoons of the hot sauce. Pour the mixture into a large resealable plastic freezer bag, and add the chicken. Seal the bag, turning it to coat the chicken, and chill at least 8 hours or up to 24 hours.

2 Whisk together the flour, pepper, and onion powder in a large bowl.

3 Cook the bacon in a large deep skillet over medium until crisp, 10 to 12 minutes. Using a slotted spoon or tongs, transfer the bacon to paper towels to drain, and discard the drippings. Finely chop the bacon.

4 Pour the oil to a depth of 2 inches into the skillet; heat the oil over high to 350°F. Remove the drumettes from the buttermilk mixture; discard the buttermilk mixture. Dredge each drumette in the flour mixture, shaking to remove the excess.

5 Fry the drumettes in the hot oil, in batches, until done, 3 to 4 minutes on each side. Drain on a wire rack over the paper towels.

6 Whisk together the mayonnaise, mustard, honey, vinegar, finely chopped bacon, and the remaining 1 tablespoon hot sauce. Serve the fried chicken drumettes with sauce.

CRISPY SPICE-RUBBED PORK BELLY BITES

It's true: Pork belly continues to be all the rage, and this appetizer is guaranteed to make you a famous host. It's terrific hot or at room temperature. Like bacon, it's also great for breakfast. Just reheat until crispy, serve with eggs any way you like them, add a side of hash, and you'll be famous with your family too. Photo page 172.

....

SERVES 12 **HANDS-ON** 20 MINUTES **TOTAL** 9 HOURS, 20 MINUTES, INCLUDING 6 HOURS, 45 MINUTES CHILLING

1   (3-pound) skinless pork belly
2   tablespoons kosher salt
2   tablespoons granulated sugar
2   teaspoons ground cumin seeds
2   teaspoons ground coriander seeds
½   teaspoon ground allspice
⅛   teaspoon ground cloves
    Honey

1 Place the pork belly on a rimmed baking sheet. Stir together the salt, sugar, cumin seeds, coriander seeds, allspice, and cloves in a small bowl. Rub the salt mixture all over the pork belly; discard any remaining salt mixture. Wrap the pork belly with plastic wrap, and chill at least 6 hours or up to 24 hours.

2 Preheat the oven to 425°F. Unwrap the pork, and place, fat side up, on a lightly greased wire rack. Place the rack on a rimmed baking sheet, and bake in the preheated oven until golden brown and crispy, about 30 minutes.

3 Reduce the oven temperature to 250°F, and cook the pork until tender when pierced with a fork, 1 hour to 1 hour and 30 minutes. Cool to room temperature, about 45 minutes. Wrap with plastic wrap, and chill until firm, 45 minutes to 1 hour.

4 Cut the pork belly into 1-inch cubes. Heat the pork in a large skillet over medium until warmed through and crispy, 3 to 5 minutes per side. Drizzle with the honey, and serve with wooden picks.

CORNBREAD-AND-LEEK PUDDING WITH PARMESAN

This recipe starts with a traditional cast-iron cornbread that is terrific on its own or with a bit of butter and honey if you wish to gild the lily. Layering the cornbread pudding keeps it all a bit less dense. Photo page 173.

SERVES 6 HANDS-ON 25 MINUTES TOTAL 2 HOURS, 20 MINUTES

CORNBREAD

- 1½ cups fine or stone-ground yellow cornmeal
- ¼ cup all-purpose flour
- 2 teaspoons granulated sugar
- 1 teaspoon baking powder
- 1 teaspoon baking soda
- 1 teaspoon kosher salt
- 1¾ cups whole buttermilk
- 2 large eggs
- 3 tablespoons salted butter

PUDDING

- 8 large eggs, lightly beaten
- 1 cup half-and-half
- 1 cup heavy cream
- 2 teaspoons kosher salt
- 1 teaspoon dried thyme
- ¾ teaspoon black pepper
- 5 ounces Gouda cheese, grated (about 1¼ cups)
- 3 ounces Parmesan cheese, grated (about 1¼ cups)
- 2 leeks
- 2 tablespoons salted butter
- 2 garlic cloves, minced

1 Prepare the Cornbread: Place a 10-inch cast-iron skillet in the oven, and preheat the oven to 450°F. Heat the skillet 7 minutes.

2 Meanwhile, stir together the cornmeal, flour, sugar, baking powder, baking soda, and salt in a large bowl. Whisk together the buttermilk and the eggs in a medium bowl.

3 Add the butter to the hot skillet, and return it to the oven until the butter is melted, about 1 minute. Stir the buttermilk mixture into the cornmeal mixture until just combined. Pour the melted butter from the skillet into the cornmeal mixture, and quickly stir to incorporate. Pour the mixture into the hot skillet, and immediately place in the oven. Bake in the preheated oven until golden brown and the cornbread pulls away from the side of the skillet, 15 to 18 minutes. Remove from the skillet, and cool completely on a wire rack, about 1 hour. Cut into 1-inch cubes. (Cornbread can be prepared up to 2 days in advance.)

4 Prepare the Pudding: Reduce the oven temperature to 350°F. Whisk together the eggs, half-and-half, cream, salt, thyme, and pepper in a large bowl; stir in 1 cup each of the Gouda and Parmesan cheeses. Set aside.

5 Remove and discard the root ends and dark green tops of the leeks. Cut in half lengthwise, and rinse thoroughly under cold running water to remove grit and sand. Thinly slice the leeks.

6 Melt the butter in a medium skillet over medium. Add the leeks, and cook, stirring occasionally, until tender, 7 to 8 minutes. Add the garlic, and cook, stirring constantly, 1 minute.

7 Place the cornbread cubes in a lightly greased 11×7-inch baking dish. Top with the leek mixture, and pour the egg mixture over the top. Sprinkle with the remaining ¼ cup each Gouda and Parmesan cheeses.

8 Bake at 350°F until the center is set, 35 to 40 minutes. Let stand 5 minutes before serving.

Pecan Vodka *recipe on page 186*

Gingerbread Bitters
recipe on page 187

FOOD GIFTS

It's always nice to have a little something homemade to give coworkers, neighbors, or the holiday party host. We have you covered in the gifts-from-scratch department.

Boozy Blue Cheese-Stuffed Olives
recipe on page 186

PECAN VODKA

The nuttiness of this infused vodka adds a toasty note to cocktails. Steep the nuts a little longer in the bottle before straining for a more pronounced pecan flavor. Photo page 184.

MAKES 6 CUPS **HANDS-ON** 10 MINUTES **TOTAL** 2 WEEKS, 10 MINUTES, INCLUDING 2 WEEKS STANDING

1   (1.75-liter) bottle vodka
3   cups pecans, toasted and cooled

1   Remove plastic pour regulator from opening of bottle. Pour 1½ cups vodka into a clean jar; seal and save for another use.

2   Create a funnel from parchment paper and masking tape, and place funnel in bottle. Gradually add the toasted pecans to remaining vodka in bottle. Seal bottle, and shake well. Store in a cool, dry place 2 weeks, shaking bottle every other day.

3   Pour the vodka through a fine wire-mesh strainer lined with cheesecloth; discard solids. Divide vodka evenly among 6 clean 1-cup glass jars. Seal tightly, and use within 1 month.

HOW TO USE: Use Pecan Vodka in a martini.

BOOZY BLUE CHEESE-STUFFED OLIVES

Salty meets saltier in this combo made in martini heaven. Photo page 185. Be sure to include the gift Gingerbread Bitters on page 187 in your gift.

MAKES ABOUT 5 ½ CUPS **HANDS-ON** 50 MINUTES **TOTAL** 50 MINUTES

2   (16-ounce) jars pitted green olives
8   ounces blue cheese, crumbled
    (about 2 cups)
¾   cup, plus 2 tablespoons gin

1   Pour the olives into a fine-mesh strainer over a bowl; reserve brine. Stuff blue cheese evenly into olives, using a wooden pick to press cheese into olives. Divide the stuffed olives evenly among 7 clean 5-ounce jars (about ¾ cup olives per jar).

2   Pour about 2 tablespoons gin into each jar. Pour reserved olive brine evenly into jars. Seal jars, and chill until ready to use. Olives will keep in refrigerator up to 1 month.

HOW TO USE: Use olives in a classic martini with a vermouth rinse and high-end gin.

GINGERBREAD BITTERS

Originally sold as medicine to be added to water to cure assorted ills, bitters have endured for the interest and depth they add to cocktails. Just a drop or two is all you need of this potent elixir to impart a warm-spiced hit of ginger to cocktails. They are especially lovely in bourbon cocktails. Photo page 185.

....

MAKES ABOUT 2 CUPS **HANDS-ON** 20 MINUTES **TOTAL** 2 WEEKS, 50 MINUTES, INCLUDING 2 WEEKS STANDING

1	cup vodka
1	teaspoon whole allspice
½	teaspoon freshly grated nutmeg
4	whole cloves
2	whole star anise
1	cinnamon stick
1	cup water
2	tablespoons molasses

1 Combine the vodka, allspice, nutmeg, cloves, star anise, and cinnamon stick in a pint jar. Seal jar, and shake well to combine. Let stand in a cool, dry place 2 weeks, shaking jar daily.

2 Pour liquid into a clean jar lined with cheesecloth or a coffee filter, reserving solids. Seal jar, and set aside.

3 Combine solids and water in a small saucepan. Bring to a boil over high, and cook, stirring occasionally, 5 minutes. Remove from the heat, and stir in molasses. Cool to room temperature, about 30 minutes.

4 Pour the molasses mixture into a large measuring cup lined with cheesecloth. Discard solids. Add vodka mixture to molasses mixture, and stir to combine. Divide evenly among 16 clean 2-ounce jars. Seal jars.

HOW TO USE: Use Gingerbread Bitters in an eggnog-meets-White Russian cocktail.

Blood Orange Marmalade
recipe on page 190

Blood Orange Marmalade

Roasted Red Pepper Jam
recipe on page 191

Preserved Lemons
recipe on page 190

Preserved
Lemons

Roasted
Red Pepper
Jam

BLOOD ORANGE MARMALADE

Orange marmalade got a makeover that is tailor-made in the perfect shade for the holidays.
Photo page 188.

MAKES 8 CUPS **HANDS-ON** 20 MINUTES **TOTAL** 1 HOUR, 30 MINUTES

2½ **pounds blood oranges, unpeeled, seeded, and finely chopped**
8 **cups water**
6 **cups granulated sugar**
¼ **cup fresh lemon juice (from 2 lemons)**

1 Combine the chopped oranges and water in a stockpot. Bring to a boil over high, and cook, stirring occasionally, until oranges are very soft, 45 minutes to 1 hour. Reduce heat to medium, and stir in sugar and lemon juice. Return the mixture to a boil, and cook, stirring constantly, until sugar dissolves. Reduce the heat to medium-low, and simmer until mixture reaches 220°F, about 10 minutes.

2 To check marmalade's consistency, place a drop of the marmalade liquid on a plate, and place in refrigerator 5 minutes. If liquid is runny, return mixture to a boil over medium, and cook, stirring often, until marmalade has thickened, checking consistency every 30 minutes.

3 Pour evenly into 8 clean 1-cup jars; cool to room temperature. Seal, and refrigerate up to 1 month.

HOW TO USE: Warm Blood Orange Marmalade, and spoon over cheesecake.

PRESERVED LEMONS

For centuries, in Morocco and in parts of the Mediterranean, brine-cured lemons have lent their concentrated lemon essence to dishes of grilled meats and tagines. In the lower zones of the South where citrus abounds, it makes perfect sense to preserve the fruit to enjoy after the harvest, plus the jars make pretty gifts. We like to use thin-skinned Meyer lemons, which are actually a cross between a common lemon and a mandarin orange. Photo page 189.

MAKES 2½ CUPS **HANDS-ON** 10 MINUTES **TOTAL** 3 WEEKS, 10 MINUTES, INCLUDING 3 WEEKS STANDING

12 **Meyer lemons, cleaned well**
½ **cup coarse sea salt**

1 Cut the lemons lengthwise into quarters, leaving ½ inch intact at the base of each lemon to hold quarters together. Place in a large bowl. Sprinkle evenly with salt. Rub salt into lemons, mashing skin and pulp to soften lemon rinds and release some juices, ensuring salt coats all surfaces.

2 Pack the lemons into 4 clean pint jars (about 3 lemons per jar). Seal jars, and let stand at room temperature 3 weeks before using.

ROASTED RED PEPPER JAM

Pepper jelly has been a holiday staple since somebody's grandma wowed a crowd with her delicious and colorful cloak for cream cheese. Now it's a whole new jam with this chunky version you can sink your teeth into. Slather it on a log of fresh goat cheese for a change of pace.
Photo page 189.

MAKES 5 CUPS HANDS-ON 30 MINUTES **TOTAL** 1 HOUR, 10 MINUTES

3 pounds red bell peppers (about
   7 bell peppers), chopped
1 jalapeño chile, seeded
   and chopped
2 garlic cloves, smashed
2 cups granulated sugar
½ cup white vinegar
1¼ cups cold water
1 teaspoon kosher salt
1 teaspoon crushed red pepper
1 (¼-ounce) envelope
   unflavored gelatin

1 Preheat broiler with oven rack 6 inches from heat. Place the bell peppers on a large rimmed baking sheet lined with aluminum foil. Broil in preheated oven, turning occasionally, until charred all over, about 6 minutes per side. Transfer bell peppers to a large bowl, and cover with plastic wrap. Let stand 10 minutes. Rub charred skins from bell peppers; discard skins, seeds, membranes, and stems. Roughly chop bell peppers.

2 Combine the roasted bell peppers, jalapeño, and garlic in a food processor; pulse until finely chopped, about 15 times.

3 Transfer the bell pepper mixture to a large saucepan. Add sugar, vinegar, and 1 cup of the cold water. Bring to a boil over medium-high, stirring often. Cook, stirring often, until sugar dissolves and bell peppers begin to break down, about 10 minutes. Remove from heat, and stir in salt and crushed red pepper.

4 Stir together the gelatin and remaining ¼ cup cold water in a small bowl. Pour gelatin mixture into hot bell pepper mixture; stir to combine. Cool to room temperature, about 30 minutes.

5 Pour the mixture evenly into 5 clean 8-ounce glass jars. Seal jars, and store in refrigerator up to 1 month.

HOW TO USE: Spoon Roasted Red Pepper Jam over a round of Brie, and serve with crostini.

HOT FUDGE SAUCE

A sundae treat, hot fudge is versatile enough to add to hot beverages or slather in a peanut butter sandwich. A spoonful added to a pot of simmering spicy chili adds depth.

MAKES 4 CUPS **HANDS-ON** 10 MINUTES **TOTAL** 1 HOUR, 10 MINUTES

2 cups granulated sugar
1¼ cups whole milk
1 cup unsalted butter
½ cup unsweetened cocoa
¼ cup all-purpose flour
1 teaspoon kosher salt
1 tablespoon vanilla extract

1 Combine the sugar, milk, butter, cocoa, flour, and salt in a large saucepan. Cook over medium-high, stirring often, until butter melts and mixture is smooth. Cook, stirring constantly, until mixture boils. Boil, stirring constantly, 1 minute. Remove from heat, and stir in vanilla.

2 Pour evenly into 4 clean 1-cup jars; let cool, about 1 hour. Seal and refrigerate up to 2 weeks.

HOW TO USE: To prepare a bourbon-mocha coffee drink, stir together 1 cup hot brewed coffee, 2 tablespoons Hot Fudge Sauce, and 2 tablespoons bourbon in a mug. Top with sweetened whipped cream and a drizzle of Hot Fudge Sauce.

BUTTERSCOTCH SAUCE

Butterscotch is basically brown sugar caramel.

MAKES 2 CUPS **HANDS-ON** 20 MINUTES **TOTAL** 1 HOUR, 20 MINUTES

¾ cup unsalted butter
2 cups packed dark brown sugar
1½ cups half-and-half
1 teaspoon kosher salt
2 teaspoons vanilla extract

1 Melt the butter in a saucepan over medium-high. Add the brown sugar; whisk until melted and combined. Whisk in the half-and-half and salt until smooth. Bring to a boil, and cook, stirring often, 5 minutes. Remove from heat, and stir in the vanilla.

2 Pour evenly into 2 clean 1-cup jars; let cool, about 1 hour. Seal and refrigerate up to 2 weeks. Serve warm.

HOW TO USE: Mix with cream cheese as a sweet dip.

SALTED CARAMEL SAUCE

A pinch of salt highlights caramel's yumminess.

MAKES 2 CUPS **HANDS-ON** 15 MINUTES **TOTAL** 1 HOUR, 15 MINUTES

2 cups granulated sugar
½ cup unsalted butter, softened
¾ cup heavy cream
2 teaspoons flaky sea salt
2 teaspoons vanilla extract

1 Place the sugar in a large saucepan. Cook over medium, stirring, until sugar melts and begins to brown, 8 minutes. Add the butter; cook, stirring, until melted and bubbly, about 2 minutes. Remove from the heat; stir in the cream, salt, and vanilla.

2 Pour evenly into 2 clean1-cup jars; let cool 1 hour. Seal and refrigerate up to 2 weeks. Serve warm.

HOW TO USE: Swirl into Greek yogurt for a treat!

VANILLA EXTRACT

Making your own vanilla is a cinch, and it's a pretty gift to give. Tuck spent vanilla pods in your sugar bowl to make vanilla sugar.

MAKES 4 CUPS **HANDS-ON** 15 MINUTES **TOTAL** 6 WEEKS, 15 MINUTES, INCLUDING 6 WEEKS STANDING

12 vanilla bean pods
4 cups vodka

Cut the vanilla bean pods in half lengthwise to expose seeds. (Do not scrape seeds.) Divide vanilla bean pods evenly among 8 clean 5-ounce jars, cutting beans as necessary to fit. Pour vodka evenly over beans, ensuring beans are completely submerged. Seal jars, and let stand in a cool, dark place at least 6 weeks, shaking jars every 3 days. Vanilla beans can be left in the jars indefinitely.

HOW TO USE: Stir Vanilla Extract into honey, and drizzle over fresh figs.

PEPPERMINT EXTRACT

This is a great addition to the baker's cabinet or the bar cart.

MAKES 1½ CUPS **HANDS-ON** 10 MINUTES **TOTAL** 3 WEEKS, 10 MINUTES, INCLUDING 3 WEEKS STANDING

2 cups loosely packed mint leaves (about 2 ounces)
1½ cups vodka

1 Place the mint leaves in a large clean jar, and use a wooden spoon to lightly bruise leaves. Pour the vodka over leaves. Seal jar, and shake to combine. Let stand in a cool, dark place at least 3 weeks, shaking jar every 3 days.

2 Pour the mixture into 3 clean 4-ounce jars lined with cheesecloth or a coffee filter. Discard solids. Seal jars.

HOW TO USE: Use Peppermint Extract instead of vanilla extract in brownie recipes.

COCONUT EXTRACT

For pure coconut flavor, don't use sweetened coconut.

MAKES 6 CUPS **HANDS-ON** 5 MINUTES **TOTAL** 4 WEEKS, 5 MINUTES, INCLUDING 4 WEEKS STANDING

2 cups unsweetened shredded coconut
6 cups vodka

1 Divide the coconut between 2 clean 1-quart jars. Top evenly with the vodka. Seal jars, and shake well to combine. Let stand in a cool, dark place at least 4 weeks, shaking jars every 3 days.

2 Pour the mixture evenly into 12 clean 4-ounce glass jars lined with cheesecloth or a coffee filter. Discard solids. Seal jars.

HOW TO USE: Use Coconut Extract instead of vanilla extract in classic chocolate chip cookies or pound cake.

HOLIDAY
INSPIRATION

CREATE A CENTERPIECE

Varying shades and heights is a design approach that rarely misses. When it comes to materials, remember to include a thriller, some filler, and a spiller in every centerpiece for balanced interest.

Hot Mulled Fruit Punch
recipe on page 115

MAKE A STYLISH SERVER

Layer napkins on a festive charger doubling as a
serving tray to beckon friends and family inside
where a warm sip awaits.

DECK THE HALLS

The open growth habit of a silvertip red fir tree allows ornaments to stand out in the linear space between branches. Accents made of felt, wool, and plaid lend a cozy warmth that is carried across settee and banister for a balanced look. A wall of pecky cypress planks provides a fitting backdrop for this foyer forest.

USE COOL COLORS

Gray, black, and silver with pops
of red and hits of nature's brown
and green are set on repeat. String
snow-frosted pinecones together to
accent the mantel.

MAKE PACKAGES PRETTY

Make your presents part of the decor by gift
wrapping with woodland elements, burlap
textures, and windowpane plaids.

TRY SOFT TONES

Pretty stockings and a graceful garland accented with pink pepperberries dress up a mantel topped with frosty trees and flickering candlelight.

CREATE A FLORAL DISPLAY

In the foyer, a concrete planter bursts with blossoms,
berries, and greenery in pink, rose, and red.

BLOOMS AND BAUBLES DISPLAY

A round tray metal tray holds an assortment of blown-glass vases filled with ranunculus and hypericum berries in varied shades of pink. Vintage-style ornaments in iridescent neutrals fill the spaces in between.

GO PINK

Don't be afraid to use nontraditional colors in your holiday decorating and wrapping. Millennial pink, anyone? Swap in pale blush tones for the usual red and add lots of silver, cream, and gold for a look that's fresh, new, and inviting. Handmade gift tags in matching colors give a personal touch.

CUSTOMIZE A WELCOME WREATH

Carry your blush tones to the door by embellishing a simple wreath with pepperberries and blush-color ribbon.

Creole Chilled Shrimp Cocktail
recipe on page 135

SERVING IDEA

Set trays of food in the rooms around your home to help with flow. Your guests will move and mingle and enjoy the festive decor as they go.

MAKE A LIVING WREATH

Deep green and variegated holly branches
stud a living ivy wreath on the door.

DEORATE WITH GREENS

A vase of lemon cypress and green hydrangea adds
a verdant touch to a bar cart in the entry that does
double duty as a catchall for gifts or favors.

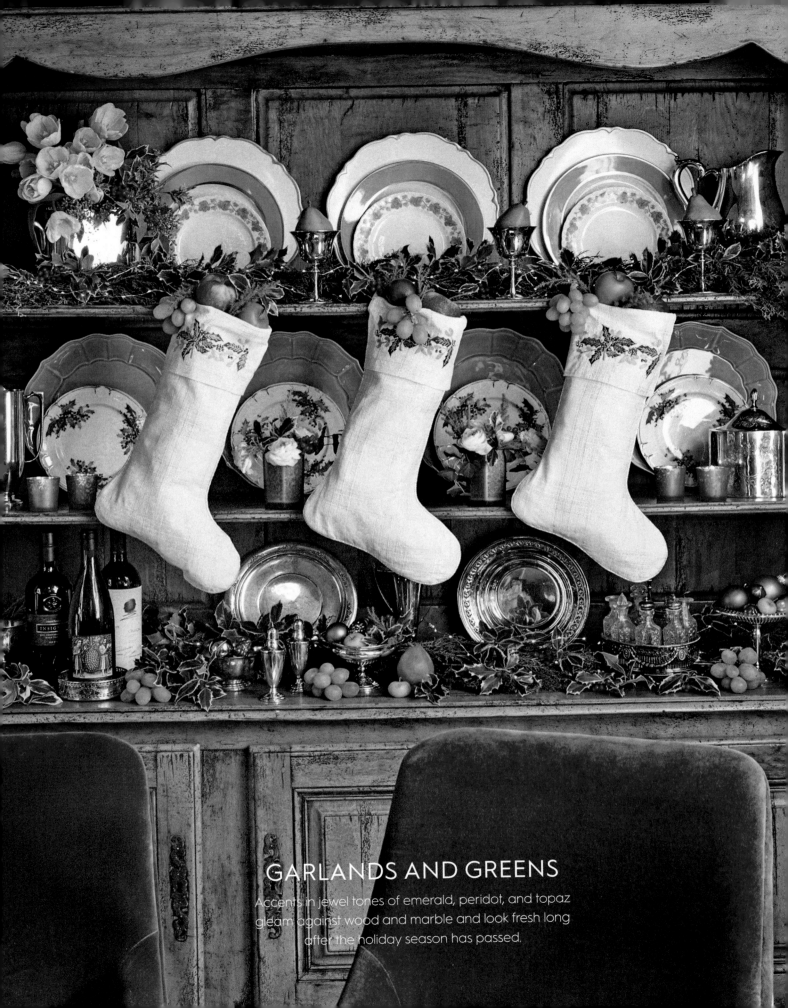

GARLANDS AND GREENS

Accents in jewel tones of emerald, peridot, and topaz
gleam against wood and marble and look fresh long
after the holiday season has passed.

DECORATE A CHAIRBACK

Gussy up often overlooked chairbacks with greenery
and ribbon to coordinate with the pretty elements on
the dining room sideboard.

PLAY WITH POPS OF RED

Few colors have as much impact as scarlet. Ruby pillows, packages, and flowers add just the right touch of Christmas to the den.

ORNAMENTAL ART

Metallic red ornaments, vintage or new,
add pizzazz to a crystal chandelier.

GO WILD

A mantel doesn't have to be festooned in stockings and icicles or lights and ornaments. Here, a lush display of greenery and clippings from the yard is secured in a damp floral foam form, which will keep the display fresh for a week or more.

FULL OF SUPRISES

A vintage tin basket filled with greenery, ornaments, and gift boxes makes a nice centerpiece or hearth decoration.

HANG AN ADVENT CALENDAR

Short on floor space? Make a wall tree out of dowel rods,
string, and decorative tin buckets. This one serves as an Advent
calendar with tucked-in surprises to be enjoyed every day of
the season.

FOLLOW THE LIGHT

A Moravian star pendant greets guests in this pretty portico draped with puddling pine boughs woven with lagoon-blue ribbon for a stunning effect.

PARTY TIME

Place noisemakers, party crackers, confetti, candy,
and all the fun stuff for guests to grab at midnight on a
tiered stand in the entry for easy access.

AFTER THE HOLIDAYS

FIRESIDE SNOW

Fill a vintage wire basket with
shimmering ornaments, faux snow,
and plant materials in shades of
blue-gray and forest green.

WINTER FROST

Frosty amaryllis bulbs bloom for weeks. Change the look after
the holidays by tucking different cuttings of greenery and
botanicals into the damp gravel that steadies the bulb.

Santa's Sipper *recipe on page 115*

Recipe Index

Pistachio- and Parmesan-Crusted Lamb Rack
recipe on page 54

Herb-Marinated Leg of Lamb
recipe on page 55

Braised Leeks with Fried Capers
recipe on page 34

Sorghum-Glazed Turnips
recipe on page 37

Raspberry-Lime Swirl Bars
recipe on page 107

Benne Seed Tuile
recipe on page 107

Spiced Rum Balls
recipe on page 105

METRIC EQUIVALENTS

The recipes that appear in this cookbook use the standard United States method for measuring liquid and dry or solid ingredients (teaspoons, tablespoons, and cups). The information in the following charts is provided to help cooks outside the U.S. successfully use these recipes. All equivalents are approximate.

Metric Equivalents for Different Types of Ingredients

A standard cup measure of a dry or solid ingredient will vary in weight depending on the type of ingredient. A standard cup of liquid is the same volume for any type of liquid. Use the following chart when converting standard cup measures to grams (weight) or milliliters (volume).

Standard Cup	Fine Powder (ex. flour)	Grain (ex. rice)	Granular (ex. sugar)	Liquid Solids (ex. butter)	Liquid (ex. milk)
1	140 g	150 g	190 g	200 g	240 ml
³/₄	105 g	113 g	143 g	150 g	180 ml
²/₃	93 g	100 g	125 g	133 g	160 ml
¹/₂	70 g	75 g	95 g	100 g	120 ml
¹/₃	47 g	50 g	63 g	67 g	80 ml
¹/₄	35 g	38 g	48 g	50 g	60 ml
¹/₈	18 g	19 g	24 g	25 g	30 ml

Useful Equivalents for Liquid Ingredients by Volume

¹/₄ tsp						=	1 ml		
¹/₂ tsp						=	2 ml		
1 tsp						=	5 ml		
3 tsp	=	1 Tbsp			=	¹/₂ fl oz	=	15 ml	
		2 Tbsp	=	¹/₈ cup	=	1 fl oz	=	30 ml	
		4 Tbsp	=	¹/₄ cup	=	2 fl oz	=	60 ml	
		5 ¹/₃ Tbsp	=	¹/₃ cup	=	3 fl oz	=	80 ml	
		8 Tbsp	=	¹/₂ cup	=	4 fl oz	=	120 ml	
		10 ²/₃ Tbsp	=	²/₃ cup	=	5 fl oz	=	160 ml	
		12 Tbsp	=	³/₄ cup	=	6 fl oz	=	180 ml	
		16 Tbsp	=	1 cup	=	8 fl oz	=	240 ml	
		1 pt	=	2 cups	=	16 fl oz	=	480 ml	
		1 qt	=	4 cups	=	32 fl oz	=	960 ml	
						33 fl oz	=	1,000 ml	= 1 l

Useful Equivalents for Dry Ingredients by Weight

(To convert ounces to grams, multiply the number of ounces by 30.)

1 oz	=	¹/₁₆ lb	=	30 g
4 oz	=	¹/₄ lb	=	120 g
8 oz	=	¹/₂ lb	=	240 g
12 oz	=	³/₄ lb	=	360 g
16 oz	=	1 lb	=	480 g

Useful Equivalents for Length

(To convert inches to centimeters, multiply the number of inches by 2.5.)

1 in					=	2.5 cm		
6 in	=	¹/₂ ft			=	15 cm		
12 in	=	1 ft			=	30 cm		
36 in	=	3 ft	=	1 yd	=	90 cm		
40 in					=	100 cm	=	1 m

Useful Equivalents for Cooking/Oven Temperatures

	Farenheit	Celsius	Gas Mark
Freeze water	32°F	0°C	
Room temperature	68°F	20°C	
Boil water	212°F	100°C	
Bake	325°F	160°C	3
	350°F	180°C	4
	375°F	190°C	5
	400°F	200°C	6
	425°F	220°C	7
	450°F	230°C	8
Broil			Grill

**Old-Fashioned
Eggnog Cheesecake**
recipe on page 68

ISBN 978-0-848-78413-3
Printed in the United States of America

First Printing 2019

Meredith Corporation

Vice President, Licensing and Brand Development: Kristen Payne
Senor Director, Licensing: Lisa DeAraujo
Licensing Coordinator: Libby Malinowski
Sales Director: Christi Crowley
Contributing Editor: Katherine Cobbs

Photographers: Greg DuPree, Victor Protasio
Contributing Photographers: Becky Luigart-Stayner, Alison Miksch
Prop Stylists: Sue Banker, Kay E. Clarke
Food Stylists: Margaret Monroe Dickey, Charles Worthington
Contributing Food Stylist: Ana Kelly
Recipe Developers and Testers: Meredith Food Studios
Senior Production Manager: Alan Rodruck

WATERBURY PUBLICATIONS
Project Editor: Lisa Kingsley
Creative Director: Ken Carlson
Senior Associate Editor: Tricia Bergman
Assistant Editor: William Bortz
Associate Design Director: Doug Samuelson
Senior Production Designer: Mindy Samuelson
Copy Editor: Terri Fredrickson
Proofreader: Gretchen Kauffman
Indexer: Mary Williams

HOLIDAY PLANNER

This handy planner will help you stay on track all season long. From decorating and table-setting tips to gift and card lists, everything you need to plan the perfect holiday is at your fingertips.

NOVEMBER 2019

Sunday	Monday	Tuesday	Wednesday
3	4	5	6
10	11	12	13
17	18	19	20
24	25	26	27

Thursday	Friday	Saturday
	1	2
7	8	9
14	15	16
21	22	23
Thanksgiving 28	29	30

HOLIDAY-READY PANTRY

Be prepared for seasonal cooking and baking by stocking up on these items.

☐ Assorted coffees, teas, hot chocolate, and eggnog
☐ Wine, beer, and soft drinks
☐ White, brown, and powdered sugars
☐ Ground allspice, cinnamon, cloves, ginger, and nutmeg
☐ Baking soda and baking powder
☐ Seasonal fresh herbs
☐ Baking chocolate
☐ Semisweet chocolate chips
☐ Assorted nuts
☐ Flaked coconut
☐ Sweetened condensed milk and evaporated milk
☐ Whipping cream
☐ Jams, jellies, and preserves
☐ Raisins, cranberries, and other fresh or dried fruits
☐ Canned pumpkin
☐ Frozen/refrigerated bread dough, biscuits, and croissants

THINGS TO DO

DECEMBER 2019

Sunday	Monday	Tuesday	Wednesday
1	2	3	4
8	9	10	11
15	16	17	18
22	23	Christmas Eve 24	Christmas Day 25
29	30	New Year's Eve 31	

Thursday	Friday	Saturday
5	6	7
12	13	14
19	20	21
Boxing Day Kwanzaa 26	27	28

GUEST-READY CHECKLIST

Impress holiday houseguests with these thoughtful gestures that will make even a den with a sofa bed seem like an upscale hotel room.

- Lavish with luxuries. Dress the bed with high-quality sheets and plump pillows. Have extra blankets readily available. Provide guests with a luggage stand, or clear space in the closet for their things.
- Create a "scentsational" ambience. Arrange a selection of scented lotions and a candle on a tray in the bedroom. Guests will appreciate a soothing lotion after a day out and about in brisk winter weather, and a fresh-scented candle will ensure a calm prelude to a long winter's nap.
- Offer good, short reads. Stack volumes of short stories, poetry, or light-hearted essays on the nightstand for relaxing bedtime reading.
- Plug in soothing sounds. Place a sound machine in the room to fill it with the peaceful lull of nature sounds, such as a babbling brook or sweet birdsong, and to drown out household hubbub. Some alarm clocks have this feature, or look for inexpensive sound machines at discount centers.
- Fashion a mini spa. In the bathroom, organize bars of soap and small bottles of shampoo and shower gel in clear apothecary jars. Provide plenty of hand towels, washcloths, and bath towels in a pretty basket.

DECORATING PLANNER

Here's a list of details and finishing touches you can use to tailor a picture-perfect house this holiday season.

DECORATIVE MATERIALS NEEDED

FROM THE YARD...

FROM AROUND THE HOUSE...

FROM THE STORE..

OTHER..

HOLIDAY DECORATIONS

FOR THE TABLE..

FOR THE DOOR..

FOR THE MANTEL..

FOR THE STAIRCASE...

OTHER..

CREATIVE GIVING

Gift giving has never been so easy! Try these creative tips when it's time to start wrapping.

Get organized. Handy over-the-door closet organizers are good for more than just keeping track of shoes. Get one with clear plastic pockets, and fill it with present-wrapping necessities. (The best part: no more disappearing scissors and rolls of tape!) Stock gift tags, ribbon, bows, box toppers, tissue paper, and even small gifts, such as candles, that you can grab at the last minute.

Adorn your gifts. Pretty up your presents by attaching bells or ornaments. Use the same-color ribbon on all your packages to make a cohesive look with different patterned wrapping papers.

Make it personal. You've found the perfect wine to bring as a hostess gift to your next holiday party, so don't just slip the bottle into a premade bag. Instead, make your gift more memorable. All you need is four or five strands of beaded wire, which you can purchase at a crafts store. Wrap the strands together to form a tiny wreath, and slide it over the neck of the bottle. Add a simple tag with a handwritten note to complete the festive look.

Get creative with gift tags. Don't bother buying more gift tags. Save money by making your own. Make color copies of tartan fabric, and cut into rectangles to create festive gift tags. Or recycle last year's Christmas cards. Cut Christmas cards into simple shapes, and use a grommet maker or hole punch to add a small hole at one end or corner. Thread twine through the hole, and tie to the gift for a creative look.

Say "Thanks for coming" with cookies. Print your favorite cookie recipe from this book on white paper or vellum, and tie it around a frozen log of the dough wrapped in parchment. When your guests are leaving, send them home with this easy Christmas gift they'll enjoy for days to come.

SIMPLE TIPS FOR A LIVING CHRISTMAS TREE

Selecting a living Christmas tree has a double bonus: You can decorate and enjoy the tree indoors, and after the holidays you can plant it outside to enjoy for years to come. Before heading to the nursery or tree lot, here are a few considerations.

Choose a tree that's right for your climate and your yard. Consider the tree's mature size, and make sure the planting area you select provides plenty of room for the tree to grow. Most conifers prefer full sun; be sure to check your tree's specific requirements.

Price will be determined by the species, size, and shearing done by the grower. Conifers that are sheared and tapered cost more than landscape-grade trees that receive no special care. Living Christmas trees can range from $30 to more than $300.

Trees are sold container-grown or balled-and-burlapped (B&B). Trees in containers weigh less and don't require potting indoors; the larger B&B trees adapt easily once planted. Unless you want a really large tree, go with a container-grown one.

When you bring your tree home, choose a decorative container (a must for a B&B tree, optional for a tree already in a container). Select one close to the size of the root ball to maintain moisture levels. Fill in any gaps with potting soil.

Place the tree away from direct heat sources, including vents, fireplaces, and kitchen stoves. A cool room (especially one with lots of natural light) is best so the tree doesn't break dormancy. Keep the tree indoors for no more than 10 days.

Water the tree daily by placing about 30 ice cubes onto the top of the root ball and letting them melt slowly. Strings of lights emit heat that can cause trees to dry out quickly, so use them for short periods of time.

To plant the tree, cut away nylon string from a B&B tree using a sharp knife if the neck of the root ball has been bound; if the material covering the root ball is nylon rather than organic material like burlap, carefully remove, as it will inhibit rooting. Lightly score the root ball with a sharp knife. Plant so the root ball is 1 to 2 inches above ground level. Where soils are heavy and clay-based, plant even higher (3 to 4 inches above ground level). Water well at planting and regularly where winters are dry. Do not fertilize if planting in winter; instead, feed in early spring.

PARTY PLANNER

Stay on top of your party plans with this time-saving menu organizer.

GUESTS	WHAT THEY'RE BRINGING	SERVING PIECES NEEDED
....	☐ appetizer ☐ beverage ☐ bread ☐ main dish ☐ side dish ☐ dessert	....
....	☐ appetizer ☐ beverage ☐ bread ☐ main dish ☐ side dish ☐ dessert	....
....	☐ appetizer ☐ beverage ☐ bread ☐ main dish ☐ side dish ☐ dessert	....
....	☐ appetizer ☐ beverage ☐ bread ☐ main dish ☐ side dish ☐ dessert	....
....	☐ appetizer ☐ beverage ☐ bread ☐ main dish ☐ side dish ☐ dessert	....
....	☐ appetizer ☐ beverage ☐ bread ☐ main dish ☐ side dish ☐ dessert	....
....	☐ appetizer ☐ beverage ☐ bread ☐ main dish ☐ side dish ☐ dessert	....
....	☐ appetizer ☐ beverage ☐ bread ☐ main dish ☐ side dish ☐ dessert	....
....	☐ appetizer ☐ beverage ☐ bread ☐ main dish ☐ side dish ☐ dessert	....
....	☐ appetizer ☐ beverage ☐ bread ☐ main dish ☐ side dish ☐ dessert	....
....	☐ appetizer ☐ beverage ☐ bread ☐ main dish ☐ side dish ☐ dessert	....
....	☐ appetizer ☐ beverage ☐ bread ☐ main dish ☐ side dish ☐ dessert	....
....	☐ appetizer ☐ beverage ☐ bread ☐ main dish ☐ side dish ☐ dessert	....
....	☐ appetizer ☐ beverage ☐ bread ☐ main dish ☐ side dish ☐ dessert	....
....	☐ appetizer ☐ beverage ☐ bread ☐ main dish ☐ side dish ☐ dessert	....
....	☐ appetizer ☐ beverage ☐ bread ☐ main dish ☐ side dish ☐ dessert	....

PARTY GUEST LIST

....
....
....
....
....
....
....
....
....
....
....
....
....
....

PARTY TO-DO LIST

....
....
....
....
....
....
....
....
....
....
....
....
....

CHRISTMAS DINNER PLANNER

Use this space to create a menu, to-do list, and guest list for your special holiday celebration.

MENU IDEAS

....
....
....
....
....
....
....

DINNER TO-DO LIST

....
....
....
....
....
....
....

CHRISTMAS DINNER GUEST LIST

....
....
....
....
....
....
....
....
....
....

PANTRY LIST

....
....
....
....
....
....
....
....
....
....
....
....
....
....

GROCERY LIST

....
....
....
....
....
....
....
....
....
....
....
....
....
....

BUNDT OFFERINGS

Bundt cakes baked in decorative pans are festive additions to holiday meals and make welcome gifts as well. You'll find baking instructions included on the packaging with most specialty pans, but because the same cake batter rises and bakes differently in each pan, keep these helpful tips in mind.

- It's important to fill pans with the correct amount of batter. If you use a smaller pan than is called for, fill it no more than one-half to two-thirds full, and reduce the bake time. Too much batter will overflow and cause the cake to collapse back into the pan. Too little batter will leave the sides of the pan exposed and shield the cake from baking evenly. So fill the pans correctly.

- Even when using the same-size pans, bake times can vary due to the density of the batter. Depending on the recipe, a cake may take as little as 45 minutes or as long as 1½ hours to bake in a 12-cup Bundt pan.

- When baking more than one cake at a time, make sure pans are similar in size. If not, bake the larger cake first, and refrigerate any remaining batter up to 1½ hours. Return batter to room temperature before baking. Refrigeration slows the activation process of leavening, but a sudden burst of hot air from the oven will quickly collapse a cold batter.

- One Bundt cake recipe fills 6 to 8 small (5×3-inch) loaf pans and usually bakes in 30 to 40 minutes. Each pan holds a little over a cup of batter, leaving just the right amount of room to add a frosting or glaze. Larger (8×4-inch) loaf pans require 50 to 60 minutes of bake time.

GIFTS & GREETINGS

Keep up with family's and friends' sizes, jot down gift ideas, and record purchases in this convenient chart. Also use it to keep track of addresses for your Christmas card list.

GIFT LIST AND SIZE CHARTS

NAME/SIZES	GIFT PURCHASED/MADE	SENT

name ....

jeans _____ shirt _____ sweater _____ jacket _____ shoes _____ belt _____

blouse _____ skirt _____ slacks _____ dress _____ suit _____ coat _____

pajamas _____ robe _____ hat _____ gloves _____ ring _____

name ....

jeans _____ shirt _____ sweater _____ jacket _____ shoes _____ belt _____

blouse _____ skirt _____ slacks _____ dress _____ suit _____ coat _____

pajamas _____ robe _____ hat _____ gloves _____ ring _____

name ....

jeans _____ shirt _____ sweater _____ jacket _____ shoes _____ belt _____

blouse _____ skirt _____ slacks _____ dress _____ suit _____ coat _____

pajamas _____ robe _____ hat _____ gloves _____ ring _____

name ....

jeans _____ shirt _____ sweater _____ jacket _____ shoes _____ belt _____

blouse _____ skirt _____ slacks _____ dress _____ suit _____ coat _____

pajamas _____ robe _____ hat _____ gloves _____ ring _____

name ....

jeans _____ shirt _____ sweater _____ jacket _____ shoes _____ belt _____

blouse _____ skirt _____ slacks _____ dress _____ suit _____ coat _____

pajamas _____ robe _____ hat _____ gloves _____ ring _____

name ....

jeans _____ shirt _____ sweater _____ jacket _____ shoes _____ belt _____

blouse _____ skirt _____ slacks _____ dress _____ suit _____ coat _____

pajamas _____ robe _____ hat _____ gloves _____ ring _____

name ....

jeans _____ shirt _____ sweater _____ jacket _____ shoes _____ belt _____

blouse _____ skirt _____ slacks _____ dress _____ suit _____ coat _____

pajamas _____ robe _____ hat _____ gloves _____ ring _____

CHRISTMAS CARD LIST

NAME	ADDRESS	SENT

HOLIDAY MEMORIES

Hold on to priceless Christmas memories forever with handwritten recollections of this season's magical moments.

TREASURED TRADITIONS

Keep track of your family's favorite holiday customs and pastimes here.

....
....
....
....
....
....
....
....
....
....
....
....
....

SPECIAL HOLIDAY ACTIVITIES

What holiday events do you look forward to year after year? Write them down here.

....
....
....
....
....
....
....
....
....
....

HOLIDAY VISITS & VISITORS

Keep a list of this year's holiday visitors. Jot down friend and family news as well.

....
....
....
....
....
....
....
....
....
....
....
....
....
....
....
....
....
....
....
....
....
....
....
....
....
....

THIS YEAR'S FAVORITE RECIPES

APPETIZERS & BEVERAGES ....
....
....
....
....
....

ENTRÉES ....
....
....
....

SIDES & SALADS ....
....
....
....

COOKIES & CANDIES ....
....
....
....

DESSERTS ....
....
....
....

LOOKING AHEAD

HOLIDAY WRAP-UP

Use this checklist to record thank-you notes sent for holiday gifts and hospitality.

NAME	GIFT AND/OR EVENT	NOTE SENT
....	....	☐
....	....	☐
....	....	☐
....	....	☐
....	....	☐
....	....	☐
....	....	☐
....	....	☐
....	....	☐
....	....	☐
....	....	☐
....	....	☐
....	....	☐

NOTES FOR NEXT YEAR

Jot ideas for Christmas 2020 on the lines below.